The Wandering Pianist

BOOKS & MORE
PIANO ISLAND PUBLISHING

The Wandering Pianist

From the Street to the Concert Hall

Congyu Wang

Published by Piano Island Publishing in 2023

This book is a memoir based on the lives, experiences, and recollections of the author over time. Some names of people, places, dates, sequences, or details of events have been changed, and some dialogues have been recreated.

The author recognizes that the opinions, perspectives, and memories of the events described in this book may differ from the different individuals involved. For avoidance of doubt, this book is not intended to injure, embarrass, or disparage ("unintentional harms") any individuals mentioned herein. While the author endeavours to avoid representations that may lead to any unintentional harms to any individuals, the author wishes to clarify that any unintentional harms ancillary to the publication of this book is purely inadvertent and wholly unintended.

First published in Singapore by

Piano Island Publishing

A CIP catalogue record for this book is available from the National Library Board (NLB) Singapore.

Hardcover ISBN: 978-981-18-8836-6

Paperback ISBN: 978-981-18-8817-5

eBook ISBN: 978-981-18-8818-2

FOREWORD

Music has a way of telling stories, of painting pictures with sound that resonate deep within us, stories that resound not just with the strings of instruments but with the hearts of those who dare to dream, persevere, and overcome. It is a great honour for me to introduce the remarkable journey of Congyu Wang, a story that encapsulates his resilience and passion as an artist.

The Wandering Pianist delves into the life of a young pianist whose unwavering dedication towards the pursuit of excellence and love of music has taken him from the challenging streets of Paris to the greatest concert halls in the world, through the path of homelessness and hardship to grand stages filled with ovations and applause.

I first met Congyu slightly over a decade ago, when he took the step to be nominated for Young Steinway Artist in Singapore. Looking back on our journey, Congyu's commitment to his craft has always been a source of inspiration for all who have had the privilege of knowing him, and his story teaches us that great accomplishments don't come from an easy path but are forged in the challenges that life throws at us. Congyu's story resonates not only in the notes he plays but in the inspiring narrative of a musician who turned adversity into artistry.

Today, Congyu stands not just as a pianist, but also as an internationally acclaimed Steinway Artist, his music and teachings reaching across borders and captivating audiences worldwide.

In the pages that follow, you will discover the highs and lows of this musician's life, the sacrifices made in pursuit of artistry, and the victory of an individual who refused to be defined by circumstances. Witness Congyu's transformation from an aspiring pianist wandering the streets of Paris into a globally sought-after pianist gracing prestigious world class venues. As the chapters unfold, you'll discover the melodies that emerged from Congyu's hardships, each note telling a story of triumph over challenges. It's a testament to the power of determination, as he navigated the challenges of pursuing music while facing the harsh realities of life. His story is not just about hitting the right notes; it's about finding the strength to continue playing when the score seems insurmountable.

Join me in celebrating *The Wandering Pianist*, a story that reminds us that even in the wandering, there is purpose, and in the music of life, every note matters.

Andrew Goh
Steinway & Sons, Thailand
Head of Operations

TO THE READER

I met Congyu almost twelve years ago at a piano event in Singapore and we reconnected again after I moved to China to work on my career. Working with him, I have come to know his story and if there is one thing that you too will learn in this book is that Congyu pursues his dreams relentlessly. His story has inspired me, and I'm sure it will also motivate and encourage you to seize control, take action, and ardently pursue your own dreams.

As you delve into the pages that follow, allow yourself to be captivated by the narrative of Congyu Wang—a musician, a friend, and an embodiment of determination and resilience.

-   *Julian Low*

When Congyu first recounted his life story to me, I immediately told him that he should write a book about it. Of course, he told me that he was already in the midst of doing so. Singaporean efficiency at its best, I joked.

Congyu never really liked the word talent. I remember him telling me that talent is one thing, but talent without hard work, perseverance, determination, and will power will not get you far. I have no doubt that he is the living proof of this. He does talk about this in his book but I do not think we will truly comprehend the sacrifices he has had to make to get to where he is today. My definition of hard work for example is definitely not the same as his.

This book isn't solely about the difficult people in his life who challenged him, brought him down, or broke his confidence, it is also about the wonderful people in his life who challenged him, inspired him, and shaped him into who he is today.

Anyone who has the honour of reading this book will, no doubt, be touched and inspired, young and old alike.

- *Rachel Leong*

To Congyu: I've cried tears in learning your story. Some for knowing just how hard it would have been on you as a teen out in the world on your own, trying to become the person you wanted to be, the person you are, and the person you are becoming. Others in celebration of your successes, big and small. Even more in hope that you become all that you aspire to be. Someone who wants it this much, who works so hard, deserves it. You deserve your dream being realised ten folds. You're an inspiration. I hope that people of all ages will read this book and be reminded of the dreams they have, or once had, and chase them.

To those who want to give up: I hope this story gives you the fuel you need to kick things into gear again and pull yourself up and keep marching on.

If you've bought this copy and don't want to give it away, get one for that person you know it will inspire. That person who you've been trying to reach but can't seem to. Sometimes all it takes is for us to see our own struggles being overcome by someone else.

This is a story for all of us. A reminder that anything is possible if we work hard, nurture our gifts and calling, and allow luck to find us. This is what Congyu did and you can do it too. Don't just enjoy reading this book, take lessons from it and share the story with others.

- **Kemone S-G Brown**

It is the author's belief that by sharing his story, readers will be able to glean their own lessons from both his deepest struggles and his greatest triumphs. I hope you enjoy what this book has in store for you. Please know that Congyu and I are rooting for you. Regardless of whatever you are facing, however down you may be feeling at the moment, whoever you are, and wherever you are, know that we are with you and for you.

- *Jesse Lai*

Contents

PROLOGUE

OVERALL, IT'S A NICE LOCATION, from the face of the building and its entrance to the interior; I suppose this is the result of being a long standing, successful broadcasting company for decades. I am very nervous as I make my way to the front desk.

"Hello, how can I help you today?" the receptionist greets me.

"Hello, I am here to see William. I have an interview at 10."

"Your name, please."

"It's Congyu Wang."

She spends a few moments scrolling down on her computer screen, then eventually says, "Oh, here we are. Okay, you can have a seat. I'll let him know that you are here."

"Thank you," I reply, and walk over to the seating area, taking a seat on the blue sofa across from the young lady who seems to also be waiting for someone. I greet her and she goes back to reading the magazine on her lap.

I scan the area but I am too nervous to think of anything else except for the interview. I hope William comes down soon and we can go get the interview on the way.

He seems to be taking a while. I am early, so I just have to sit here. I try to read through my emails but I can't focus. I've had many interviews before but this one will be live and very important, so I want it to go well.

I check the time on my phone; he still has time before we start.

He's walking towards me now. I stand up immediately. He smiles and I smile back. "Hi 'Kongyou,' I'm William."

"Hi William, nice to meet you," I reply, hoping that I am hiding the fact that my nervousness just increased by a thousand percent well.

"Did you find the place easily?"

"I used an Uber. Seemed straightforward." He chuckles. "Is it usually hard to find?"

"Depends on who you ask. We've had people call multiple times on the way because they get lost."

"Guess I got a good driver then."

"Guess you did." We both laugh. "Okay, I'll get you a visitor's pass and we can head on up. We still have a few minutes, so we can quickly go over some things before the show starts."

"Sure," I say, and we walk back to the receptionist who asks me to sign a form then hands me a lanyard with a visitor's pass attached to it.

William leads the way as we make our way to the lift. We get in.

"Okay, for starters, how do you pronounce your name? Is it Kongyou or Songyou? My co-host thinks it's a French name and suppose it's Kongyou like 'con' in French?"

Oh yes. I heard him right a few moments ago. "No, not Kongyou. Con means idiot in French, so I wouldn't be happy with my parents if they gave me a French name with con in it."

I laugh and he joins in, agreeing it makes sense.

"It's a Chinese name. Congyu. You pronounce it like there is a 'Ts' instead of a 'C' at the beginning, and it's like saying 'the German 'ü' at the end instead of 'you.' Like a rounded 'ew' in English. More like Tsongew," I keep my lips tightly rounded for the 'ew' at the end.

"Hmm. So, it's Songew." He's not rounding his lips enough and he's still missing the 'Ts' pronunciation.

I laugh. "No, it's Tsongew."

"It's quite difficult to say. So, it's spelt Songyou or Kongyou but pronounced Songew."

"The spelling is correct. It's just the pronunciation that's not right."

"Tsongyou. Songyou..." he tries again. "It's difficult to say it."

"Maybe try saying it a bit more slowly."

"Tsongyou."

"That's close. Just need a little work on the end."

We continue this for a while before he finally gets close enough. It's making me far more nervous and I am sure I will mess up the interview if I go into it with so much nerves, so I finally tell him that he's got it, though he still says 'you' at the end of my name.

I am trying to focus on something he's trying to clarify before the interview but my thoughts circle back to the dilemma that has plagued me for as long as I can remember—the enigma of my name. Why is it so intricate that so many people find it challenging to read my name correctly? My friends, my teachers, and now this interviewer.

Intelligent King

I came through the door, weary from a long day at school, and was instantly captivated by the aroma of my mother's cooking. The scent wrapped around me, as comforting and familiar as a mother's embrace. One that I would have done well with then.

I made my way straight to the kitchen, my footsteps heavy with the weight of my concerns. The savoury fragrance of her homemade noodles filled the air, but today, they served as mere background music to the question that had been plaguing me all the way home. My mother's cooking had the power to soothe my soul, but right then, it was my heart that needed comforting, and only an answer could provide that solace.

I sat across from my mother at our kitchen table.

"What's wrong? Did something happen at school?"

"Mummy," I began, my voice trembling with a mixture of frustration and confusion, "why did you give me such a silly name? My teacher keep saying Kongyou when she marks the register and the entire class laughs at me. She can't pronounce my name right!"

"Your name isn't a silly name. It's a good name. They're laughing because their names aren't as nice. You should tell the teacher how to say your name."

"I do but she still can't say it right. It's a silly name. Everyone says it's a silly name."

"It's not; I promise you. It's a very special name because you are a very special boy," she said.

"How can it be special if no one can pronounce it?"

"It is. Cong means 'intelligent' in Chinese, and Yu means… Well, the very first Chinese Dynasty was called Xia Dynasty and their very first king was Yu the Great. He was a very successful emperor. So, we named you after him. We want you to grow up to be intelligent and wise, like the emperor."

"Huh?"

Her words, although well-intentioned, offered little comfort. My tears flowed freely, and I struggled to grasp the wisdom she sought to convey. How could such a name, supposedly rich with potential, be the biggest source of endless teasing and frustration? The weight of my name felt more like an anchor. It was holding me back rather than propelling me forward. What was the point? If no one could read my name, what use was its meaning?

The more I contemplated, the more it felt like an unfair burden. I did not want this name. Why couldn't she have called me David or something simple and easy to read.

CHAPTER 1

MY CONCERT STARTS IN A few hours, so I've decided to take a stroll through the beautiful Italian village where I have been staying for the last two days and will stay for another three. I have practiced the piece enough times; the break is much needed.

I close the gate and step onto the charming street that borders the quaint Italian courtyard. The air buzzes with the sounds of the village in the afternoon: children playing joyfully in the narrow alleys, their laughter echoing off the ancient stone walls, while the distant hum of Vespas and the occasional chime of church bells weave a harmonious melody that feels as timeless as the village itself.

It's a beautiful, warm summer's day, with the azure sky stretching endlessly overhead, painted with wisps of bright, white clouds that drift lazily, casting fleeting shadows on the sun-dappled streets below. I make my way through the winding cobblestone alleys of this picturesque Italian village, each twist and turn revealing a new layer of its timeless charm. I have not been to this village before, but the people greet me as if I am one of their own. They all seem to know that I have rented the cottage from Alonzo, and they know exactly why I am here; though I haven't seen any flyers or adverts around yet. A few mentioned yesterday that they will be attending the piano concert that I will be playing at.

After walking for about 20 minutes, I have made it to the square. It is much noisier than the street I am staying on. The square teems with life and resonates with a symphony of sounds. Conversations in rapid Italian fill the air, a harmonious cacophony that seems to blend seamlessly with the cheerful melodies played by a local street musician, his accordion breathing life into the village. Laughter, both hearty and carefree, spills from the tables of the old-fashioned cafés that line the square, where villagers and visitors alike savour coffee and gelato.

I inhale deeply, and the aroma of freshly baked bread and simmering tomato sauce from nearby trattorias dances around me, mingling with the sweet fragrance of blooming jasmine vines adorning wrought-iron balconies. The earthy scent of the village's centuries-old stone walls, warmed by the sun, blends with the faint breeze carrying hints of the nearby olive groves. My stomach grumbles, and I glance at my wristwatch; it's indeed time for lunch. As I stroll through the square, I notice a charming little restaurant across the way. It's different from the café where I dined yesterday, and curiosity beckons me to give it a try. With each step, the sun's warm embrace and the lively ambiance of the village envelop me.

I'm about to reach the restaurant's entrance when a heartwarming scene unfolds before me. My eyes meet those of a local man sitting at a nearby table, his young son happily savouring an ice cream cone beside him. In this moment that captures the essence of parenthood, the ice cream tumbles from the child's grasp, splattering onto the cobblestones. The boy's face contorts into a pout, and he cries out, "Papà! Papà!"

His father, quick to respond, scoops him up with tenderness, comforting the young boy. Without hesitation, the father heads back to the ice cream cart, determined to remedy the situation. My heart swells with emotion as I witness this simple, loving gesture. There's no scolding, no frustration—only genuine care and a father's immediate effort to meet his son's need.

I find myself frozen in my tracks, the scene unfolding before me like a poignant painting. It strikes a chord deep within me, transporting me back to my own childhood—a time when my tears were met with annoyance rather than understanding, especially by my own father. The stark contrast between then and now leaves me emotionally stirred.

My Formative Years

There are a few things that I want you to know off the bat. I think they will help you understand who I am as a pianist and how I have become the person I am today. The first is that I am not a special kid. I wasn't exceptionally gifted. Playing the piano didn't come naturally to me. I wasn't naturally smart or hard working at school either. I also had a childhood where I experienced a lot of trauma, where my feelings didn't matter, and that led me to become very overprotective, and not just of myself. I get very possessive with things and people; I don't like to experience loss of any kind. In all honesty, I don't truly understand why that is but it might be attached to the things I went through while growing up; and simply how my life was, which was quite different to many people's.

My first loss, although I don't remember the feeling I experienced, was at the age of four when I lost my grandfather. My mother is the first child of five children and I was the first grandson. Being Chinese, having a boy child is something they take pride in, so my mother's family was very proud when my mother gave birth to me. My grandfather took a liking to me. Although I was only two or three when it started, I have vivid memories of us being really close.

My grandfather was a diabetic and would have to go to dialysis. He would come to get me after dialysis and we would go out and have a meal together or he would take me to get ice-cream or something. I remember very clearly, a day when he came to get me at the house and I was taken to meet him by our maid, Mary. She took me to meet him downstairs and we went to the food court. If there was one thing about my grandfather, it was that if he wanted something, he wanted it now. He was a stubborn man who had to have his way. That day, I was going to find out how dangerous that can be.

I didn't want to eat. I had already eaten lunch at home and was full. My grandfather didn't want to hear that, though. He ordered barley for himself and porridge for me. He just wanted us to have lunch together, and that meant I had to eat something. I must have been about three and a half at the time but it left a deep impression on me. Here I was extremely full from the lunch I had eaten earlier but I was being asked by my grandfather to eat again. Even though I told him I had already eaten, he insisted that I eat with him. Eventually, I ate the porridge, and before you knew it, I was vomiting. The vomiting started and I couldn't stop. Even as Mary walked me home, I vomited all the way there.

I remember this clearly because I found it embarrassing. To this day, I still have visions of this incident—it even replays in my dreams—though I was so young at the time. I think it stays with me because it not only sums up who my grandfather was but is also a symbol of the pressure cooker that I lived in from a very young age and how, if I didn't get out of it, I would combust.

I loved the times my grandfather would play with me, tickle me, and just make time for me. I loved spending time with him. That day, however, I learned that he was very demanding.

Later in life, I found out that he was a heavy drinker and smoker. It was also when I was much older that I found out that he was addicted to gambling. Still, when he was alive, all I knew of him was that he liked me and he liked spending time with me. Learning about his flaws didn't change the fact that I enjoyed my time with him. Although I had this negative experience with him, I still know for a fact that he loved me. Everyone knew that he loved his grandson.

The day he passed is also one I can remember clearly. I was at school playing with some friends when my mother appeared to take me home. I went to the hospital to see my grandfather for the last time. The last words he spoke to me were, "Listen to your mother. Be good to your mother." A request I continue to try to honour to this day. There were a lot of people around his death bed weeping and I just watched them without truly understanding that he was dying. I didn't understand what death was. I was a child, only four years old at the time, so I didn't really grasp what was happening. Even when we went to his wake and he was in the coffin, I still didn't comprehend that he was gone forever.

The loss of my grandfather was the very first loss in my life but I don't think that it played any role in me being the possessive person that I am now. The interesting thing is that I wasn't attached to him. I didn't understand why but it could be because I found out much later, while I was in school, that my mother kept me from getting too close to him because of his addiction. My mother had boundaries in place and tried to protect me from following in the same footsteps.

I was raised primarily by my mother. She was always there, and for the first few years of my life, I was very attached to her. My mother was my whole world in so many ways. I never imagined us being separated from each other in any form. She often says that I would follow her around everywhere she went when I was a child, which I do remember. As for my father, I didn't have a great relationship with him.

From the day I was born, my father only came home on Tuesdays and Fridays each week. Every two weeks, he would come home on Sunday as well. He was never a constant in my life. Each year, we would have school events, events where parents were present for their children. My mother would always show up but my father was never there. Even up to this point in my life, where I have played over a thousand recitals or concerts, my father has never been present. He has never seen me play.

I must have been about nine years old when I was given a form at school to fill in. We were having a moon lantern festival at school and my parents' names needed to be filled in on the form so they could participate. We were going to be having games and everyone needed to be on the list. Even though I carry my father's surname, I realised that day that I didn't know my father's name. I didn't really know who my father was. I could easily fill in my mother's details but I had no idea what my father's first name was. I didn't know his national identity number, even though I knew my mother's. This was the first time I realised the mystery that my father is. Much later in life, though, I would get a far better understanding, and things would make more sense.

I never had a good relationship with my father. He was very cold towards me, and his disapproval seemed to have taken root as early as I could remember. I was, undeniably, a cry-baby during my formative years, and my father played a significant role in that aspect of my personality. To him, it seemed that I would just find reasons to cry. He never took the time to try to understand what was wrong. From scraped knees to forgotten toys, from the thunder's roar to the slightest reprimand, or even just out of the blue, I would cry. Sometimes, when I look back on those years, I think that my young heart craved comfort and reassurance, but my father's response was far from soothing. Instead of offering consolation, he would resort to harsh methods—a pinch here, a disapproving glance there, or an occasional spanking—anything to amplify my tears, as if my crying were an affront to his very being.

It was painfully clear that he never liked me, an undeniable truth etched into every memory of my childhood. He was never the loving, nurturing figure I longed for; he remained a distant, intimidating presence. The scars of his emotional neglect ran deep, leaving me with a sense of inadequacy and yearning for the warmth that had always eluded our relationship.

I felt like my mom, siblings, and I were more like his servants than his family. Whenever he was coming home, we would have to put on a show, making sure everything was perfect for him. Our home had to be in immaculate condition. We would have to prepare tea, put his shoes aside nicely, and do everything he wanted. It felt like we were being visited by a distinguished guest as opposed to my father coming home. The mere prospect of his weekly return home was fraught with trauma. Once home, he became an unwelcome presence that cast a shadow over me. The anticipation of his arrival was a relentless source of dread, each week carrying the ominous promise of re-traumatization, which was too much to deal with as a small child.

I could never regard him as a role model because my fear of him overshadowed any semblance of admiration. Whenever my father cast his gaze upon me, I didn't bask in the warmth of paternal love; instead, I felt the weight of his judgments bearing down on me. In his eyes, I was perpetually inadequate, forever falling short of his elusive standards. I was never good enough, constantly haunted by the spectre of being less than the perfect child and student he expected me to be.

Unfortunately, both my parents saw excelling at academics as the most important thing, and I couldn't give them that. At the end of each semester at school, we would have to take home our report cards for our parents to sign. This presented me with some of the most traumatic days in my childhood. I would be completely distressed. On these days, I wouldn't want to go home. I'd wished that something could happen to make the report card go away, so I wouldn't have to face my parents. I had to go through this from the age of eight to fifteen and it was awful. They were never happy with my grades. They had extremely high expectations and my results never matched up. I have a sister who is two years older than me and we were constantly compared from very early on in my life. She was the top student in school, while I did not do well enough for them. There were consequences.

In Singapore, beating your children is not against the law. My parents kept a cane at home, so you can imagine what they would do to me if I did poorly at school. Eventually, the caning stopped and they started with the verbal and psychological abuse. Everything they had to say to me was from a comparison perspective. So often, my mother or father would say, "Why can't you be like your sister? Why can't you be more like her?" Imagine being told that over and over again throughout your entire childhood by your own parents.

As much as my father didn't like me and was cold to me, he was also not my favourite person by any means. I did everything I could to avoid his presence. If I wasn't seen, then he couldn't make me feel as horrified as I did when he was at home. When my father was around, he hated to see me doing anything except things that involved a book. Playtime, the joyful essence of childhood, was forbidden in his eyes. If he ever caught me engaged in anything resembling play, his stern voice would command me to fetch a book, to immerse myself in the world of academia without respite. He wanted me to be studious. To focus on nothing but school. I always had to be studying, nothing else. For seven years, he was the most dreaded person on the planet. With every passing semester, the dread would intensify, for I knew that his 'discipline' awaited me—a harsh reminder of the academic standards he relentlessly imposed, standards that I perpetually struggled to meet.

I suppose he realizes that I am staring, lost in my thoughts, because he waves at me, a friendly smile breaking across his face. His small gesture of recognition pulls me out of my reverie, grounding me back in the present moment. Blinking away the memories of my own past and my distant father, I return the smile and wave back, suddenly feeling a deeper connection with this kind, caring father and his son. The weight of my own past still lingers, but for now, it's pushed to the periphery of my thoughts.

With a renewed sense of purpose, I make my way into the charming restaurant. The aroma of freshly baked bread and simmering tomato sauce that had tantalized my senses from outside is much stronger. It's a cozy, rustic trattoria with checkered tablecloths and the soft glow that resembles candlelight.

I find a quiet corner and settle into a comfortable chair. My eyes scan the menu, and I decide to start with a classic Caprese salad, a medley of plump, ripe tomatoes, creamy mozzarella, fresh basil leaves, and a drizzle of olive oil. For the main course, I opt for a plate of homemade tagliatelle al tartufo, delicate ribbons of pasta topped with a decadent truffle cream sauce, a dish as rich and indulgent as the memories I've left outside.

As the waiter approaches to take my order, I briefly consider indulging in a glass of red wine to accompany my meal. The thought lingers momentarily, but then, I decide against it. Wine can wait; I'll likely have a glass tomorrow when I go out to celebrate.

Me as a one year old; the t-shirt says it all.

With my maternal grandmother

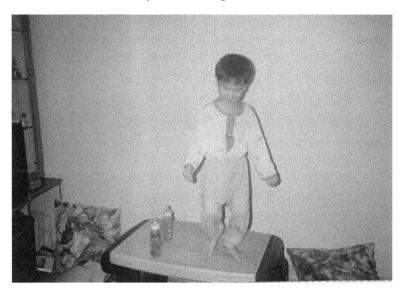

At home at age three

CHAPTER 2

I STAND BY THE WINDOW of my classroom, a haven of music and learning, where young minds embark on their journeys into the world of piano. It's a place where dreams take root, and today, I have the privilege of witnessing a new beginning.

The distant hum of voices and footsteps grows closer, and I hope that it is the arrival of my newest student. I glance at my watch; it's a moment past our scheduled time. Just as a flicker of concern crosses my mind, the classroom door swings open, and a young boy of eight bursts in. His face, alight with excitement, is a portrait of youthful enthusiasm. He greets me with a quick, "Bonjour!" before squirming out of his mother's grasp.

I chuckle at his boundless energy, appreciating the eagerness with which he approaches the piano, the instrument that I suppose will soon become his muse. His eyes dart around the room, taking in the piano's gleaming keys, the neatly arranged sheet music, and the warm, inviting atmosphere. In an instant, he's seated at the piano bench, fingers hovering over the keys as if they were old friends.

I approach him with a warm smile, extending a hand in greeting. "Bonjour! Je m'appelle Congyu," I say, introducing myself to this young musical adventurer. His name, he tells me, is Julien, and he beams with pride as he pronounces it. Julien's zest for music is palpable, and it's clear that this is a special day for him. As he begins to explore the piano's keyboard, I can't help but feel inspired by his unbridled curiosity.

Standing next to me, Julien's mother bears a warm smile that mirrors her son's enthusiasm. I can sense her pride in Julien's newfound appetite for the piano. We chat briefly and she shares the story of his relentless begging for piano lessons, a plea she's now being able to fulfil.

Her eyes reflect a mix of hope and concern as she confides in me. "Last year, he was obsessed with the cello," she says. "He begged me for lessons, and I arranged them for him. But, after a few months, he lost interest and stopped wanting to go." She looks at Julien, who's now fully engrossed in pressing keys on the piano.

I meet her gaze with empathy and reassurance. "It's wonderful that you support his curiosity and passions," I tell her. "Children have a way of exploring the world and discovering their interests. It's all a part of their journey. Who knows, Julien might find that the piano is his true calling, or perhaps it will be something else. What's important is that he has the opportunity to explore and find what resonates with him."

Her eyes soften with gratitude, and she nods in understanding. "Thank you for that reassurance," she says.

"My friends think I am spoiling him but I just want him to have the chance to explore and find his passion."

For a split second, her face turns into my mother's. I blink my eyes quickly, keeping myself in this moment. I look back at Julien. I can't help but feel a deep sense of fulfilment. Today marks the start of a musical journey for this young boy, and as his teacher, I have the honour of helping him figure out if it's his true calling.

"Allowing him to find out who he really is as a person is not spoiling him. Don't listen to your friends on that one," I tell her and she smiles an even warmer smile than before.

My First True Love

I knew I hated traditional schooling from the very young age of five. I remember very vividly the moment I decided that school itself was not for me. Of course, my parents' constant high expectations and demands didn't help.

It was December 1997. At that tender age, I was already having tuition. I was never a trouble maker whether at school or at home. I wasn't that child who would be disciplined by teachers. Yes, I would be disciplined by my parents but that's an entirely different story. In school, I knew to be on my best behaviour; otherwise, I would get into trouble at home and that was a big no. Whatever task I was asked to do, I would do. Wherever I was meant to be at whatever time, according to what my teacher said, I would be there. I just wasn't a child who got into trouble. My teacher never had to ridicule me in class. I was almost invisible.

Now, here I was at five years old being chased by a boy called Isaac. He was a crazy kid with a lot of excess energy. He started chasing me and I had to run to get away from him. All of a sudden, he fell; he fell really hard onto the concrete floor on his head. The next thing I knew, I was in the principal's office with him, the principal, and the class teacher. The atmosphere was charged with accusation, and every gaze seemed to point squarely at me. I had only been trying to escape from Isaac's relentless chase, yet now, I found myself unjustly held responsible for the harm he had inflicted upon himself. My attempts to explain, to defend my innocence, fell on deaf ears. No matter what I said or did, I wasn't being believed.

In that pivotal moment, I had a disheartening revelation—an unsettling glimpse into a school system seemingly indifferent to the pursuit of truth and the safety of the children entrusted to its care. It was a system ready to appease those in authority, willing to craft convenient answers regardless of their veracity. In this instance, they needed an answer for Isaac's parents, and I had been chosen as the scapegoat.

What struck me, even at such a young age, was the persistence of our teacher—who couldn't even pronounce my name—repeatedly labelling me as a troublemaker. She uttered the accusation with such conviction, asserting that I must have pushed Isaac. Her certainty was baffling, considering she hadn't witnessed the chase, the fall, or my desperate attempts to get away from Isaac.

In that office, while everyone blamed me for something I hadn't done, I felt utterly powerless. I knew that my troubles wouldn't end with the school's judgment. I knew I was going to get into trouble at home. My parents wouldn't believe me; they didn't. I will always remember this night where I was disciplined for all the wrong reasons. I just wasn't believed by anyone and Isaac didn't tell the truth.

It has nothing to do with education itself as such but this scarred me as it made me understand that school wasn't for me. It wasn't a safe place. As I got older, it was confirmed even more. Between my parents comparing me to my sister and school not being a place where they cared about the truth, it made me think that I just didn't want to be there, and it showed. I wasn't failing miserably but I was never able to live up to my parents' academic expectations.

I spent so much of my young life being forced to think that without doing well in school, I just wouldn't be anything. From very early in my life, this idea that I would have to settle for some low paying job because I wasn't a genius or smart enough was forced upon me. Yet, something inside me refused to believe this, so I kept looking for something else, to become something that wasn't so heavily dependent on me doing exceptionally well in traditional school.

When I completed my Primary School Leaving Exanimation (PSLE), which I didn't do 'exceptional' in, I chose a school that was not far from my home. At that point in time, I had come up with this grand idea that I would become a badminton player. Not only would this be something that I enjoyed, but it would also help me gain respect from my family and peers at school, and then later in life. No low level paying job for me; I was going to become a badminton star. So, I chose this school because they had a badminton team that was pretty decent. This was my first choice of six options and I was very lucky to be chosen to attend Fairfield Methodist Secondary School. I didn't get into the express route—I wasn't as smart as my sister. I had to go the academic route, which meant I would be in school for five years instead of four.

I wasn't a bad student because I wasn't smart. I just didn't like school. Education was surrounded by drama both at school and at home. Nevertheless, I suppose everything has its place and being at Fairfield Methodist Secondary School was where I was meant to be at that time. It is amazing how we get pulled in the exact direction that we are meant to as we go through life. At this school, where I wanted to play badminton and become a great sportsman, I was about to be pulled onto the actual road I was meant to be treading.

I heard that the chapel at my school was looking for a pianist to join their band for the Tuesday chapel services. Of course, me being me, I bragged my way into it. I told them that I had a nice piano at home, that I had been playing from the age of three—two pieces of information which were true. However, I added that I was playing at Grade 8. At the time, I was playing good—definitely not that good—but I wanted to play and I had to convince them that I was the best choice. I decided that a little bragging wouldn't hurt.

My father was the breadwinner of our family, and he excelled at providing for us financially. That much I can't deny. Although, when it came to helping me pursue my dreams of becoming a concert pianist, his contributions were notably absent. With my sister needing to practice the piano, my father bought a Ronisch Upright Piano for the house, which was a substantial investment in those days. My sister was a very good pianist from a young age. Whenever my sister played, he showered her with praise, his eyes lighting up as he immersed himself in the music. Her talent was undeniable. I, on the other hand, wasn't as good of a pianist, and my father made sure to tell me.

38

I wrongly believed that the piano was reserved for girls, an assumption I carried with me into my early years. Consequently, I didn't invest much effort in becoming a proficient player. It didn't help that my father thought I was a useless player either. Regardless of this fact, however, and the fact that I hadn't sat for my Grade 8 exam yet, I was going to get into that band—and joined the band I did.

Even though I had started playing in the band, I still wanted to play badminton; I mean, it was cool. I wanted to be a cool badminton player. I was very good at playing badminton, plus I was still a stereotypical thinking male who thought that the piano was for girls. I soon realised that it had its perks, however.

Now, I was a teenager going through puberty. During primary school, I had gained a lot of weight. Everything was too much. Being bullied at school, not liking school in general, and going through so much at home, I had used food to soothe my feelings. However, I wanted to have a completely different experience in secondary school, so I lost a lot of weight and looked much better than I did in primary school. I thought it would be cool to play badminton and get all the attention and affirmation from my peers at this new school. I definitely looked different. I wasn't bad looking. With puberty raging, I wanted attention from girls, too. Playing badminton offered that, but I got even more when I also started playing the piano—something I didn't expect.

Even with all the positive attention playing the piano got me, my gift and love for the piano only started shining through after I joined the Christian band at school. This was ultimately influenced by my piano teacher. When I started playing the piano at three and a half, I wasn't able to find a good teacher because I had trouble understanding what they were talking about when they spoke music lingo. I didn't understand what a crochet or semiquaver was. My mother told me that I changed five teachers within the span of six months because I wasn't able to understand anything. It was only when I met Madam Chew, who was also my sister's teacher, that I settled down with playing the piano. My mother admired her because she was patient with children. I studied the piano with Madam Chew from the age of six to thirteen.

I think she's a great piano teacher for kids who are not thriving to become concert pianists. If you want to train to only be graded, to achieve a Grade 8, she's the best person to go to. When I studied with her, she wasn't interested in training students for anything outside of passing the piano exams. She was very strict and to the books. You weren't allowed to experiment and explore different pieces. For her, a student was only to come in and play their exam pieces and go home; nothing more, nothing less.

I was already playing *La Campanella* by Franz Liszt and more advance pieces such as the *Fantasy Impromptu* by Chopin—ones that were more difficult than the graded pieces—but Madam Chew didn't want to hear any of it. She wanted me to stick to the standard exam pieces. I realised that I wasn't able to grow any further with her. I wanted to play different pieces and to improvise, which I wasn't able to do with her. I told my mother and she decided that Madam

Chew was no longer the right teacher for me. She'd heard from her friends that there was a piano school called Sylvia Ng Piano Studio where the Indonesian born, American concert pianist, Sylvia Ng taught. It's a private school and my mother got me into it.

I didn't go straight to Sylvia for classes. I wasn't up to the standard that she taught. Up to this point, I was only a Grade 7, although I'd been bragging that I had a Grade 8. At the age of thirteen and playing at Grade 7, it wasn't something to be proud of. The thing is that I never really cared about the exam grades in the sense of taking and passing the exams. I knew that it was never going to make me a better person or pianist. I knew that bragging about having a high grade gave me respect and opportunities but I wasn't hung up on the exams or the grades themselves.

I was taught by Mr Jean Yip, whom Sylvia had assigned to teach me. The very first person who really changed my life and transformed my perception of the piano. From the moment I started studying with Mr Jean Yip, I realised that the piano was not just for girls. With Mr Jean Yip, I learned that the piano was not a simple instrument. I felt as though he put life into my playing. It was as if I had been playing the piano wrong all along and he taught me how to use it properly and what its value was. I learned to see the instrument for the beauty that it is.

Although Mr Jean Yip was somewhat like Madam Chew as he would often want to stick to teaching me pieces at my grade, he was different in that, if I paid him more, he would teach me above my grade. It was Mr Jean Yip who taught me my first Chopin nocturne, the last piece of music to be broadcasted in Poland before the German invasion in World War II. I enjoyed his lessons and took them very seriously. I didn't want to disappoint him. In my mind, I wanted to grow up to play like him. He was inspiring. These were possibly the best times I had as a piano student.

Unfortunately, things did not end well with Mr Jean Yip. I only studied with him for a year. I got too ambitious too quickly. He would be teaching me a piece and I would be learning that and other pieces on my own. I was learning pieces that were far too difficult for me at the time and he decided that it was time for me to look for another piano teacher. In his opinion, I was becoming too arrogant. Mr Jean Yip lit a quiet confidence inside of me as a pianist, though: He always said I was talented and would tell my mother and other students that I was going to be a great pianist one day.

When Mr Jean Yip decided to stop teaching me, I started studying with Sylvia. As the head of the school, I thought she would be a fierce and strict teacher, but she wasn't. She was the kindest teacher ever.

Mr Jean Yip had given me a ticket to go see Yevgeny Subin who was playing *Tchaikovsky Piano Concerto No. 1* at the Esplanade Concert Hall. Subin played beautifully, and this concert changed the trajectory of my entire life. I wanted to become a concert pianist. The seed was planted. Now a student of Sylvia, it seemed that this was going to be possible for me. Sylvia would organise many piano classes where students could perform for each other. She didn't just focus on passing exams. She taught us how to be musicians, which was just what I wanted at the time. She taught her students how to play for concerts, and the idea that I could become a concert pianist started to find root.

The second thing that drove me to wanting to play the piano was the movie, *The Pianist*. I remember staying up to watch this three-hour film into the wee hours of the morning. It was back then when we didn't have Netflix and other non-commercial interrupting apps. I would watch *The Pianist* every time it would come on television. It was also because of this movie that I found a deeper connection with Mr Jean Yip while he was teaching me Chopin's *C sharp minor Nocturne*.

Secondary school was more or less a good experience in the first two years because of my discovery of the piano and my gift for the instrument. For once in my life, I felt that I had a purpose. Of course, I started bragging even more. So much so that every time there was a special event at school like Racial Harmony Day, Father's Day, All Saints Day—whatever the day, you name it—they would always organise some kind of students performance and I would always have a part to play in it. They always found a way to include me in the programme. I would often be listed as "Future Great Pianist" and the sorts. Even so, I still wasn't sure that I was going to become a pianist. I had realised that this was what I wanted to be if not a badminton player, but I didn't know if I was going to become one. I believed everyone when they said that I would never achieve anything in my life.

Me sitting at our home piano at the age of four or five

CHAPTER 3

SEATED INSIDE A HELICOPTER SOARING above the breathtaking Kruger National Park, the sounds that surround me transform into a masterpiece of their own, each note resonating with the grace and complexity of piano music. It is not a classical piece though; I'd more liken it to Romanian folklore.

The rhythmic thrum of the helicopter's rotor blades, as they slice through the air with precision, becomes the deep bass notes of a grand piano, grounding the composition with their powerful resonance. It's a steady heartbeat, setting the tempo for our aerial journey.

The engines' symphonic hum, harmonizing with one another, takes on the qualities of a duet between two skilled pianists, each note perfectly synchronized. The music they create is a testament to the mechanical prowess of this flying machine, melody that dances through the cabin like a musical conversation.

We gain altitude, and the world below begins to unfold, much like the opening of a grand piano lid, revealing the rich landscape of the Kruger National Park. The diverse soundscape of the park—the calls of wild animals, the rustling of leaves, the rushing of water—blend seamlessly into the composition. It's as if nature herself is contributing to this impromptu performance, adding layers of complexity and depth.

The wind rushing past the helicopter's fuselage becomes the delicate trills of piano keys, adding a touch of whimsy to the symphony. I close my eyes and immerse myself in this auditory masterpiece, I can't help but draw parallels to the piano music I have played throughout my life. The helicopter's flight path mirrors the ebb and flow of a musical composition, with crescendos and decrescendos that mirror the rise and fall of notes.

Now I gaze out of the helicopter's window, and the landscape below shifts, revealing the vibrant and diverse ecosystem of Kruger National Park. The sounds of wildlife— the trumpeting of elephants, the chirping of birds, the distant roar of lions—now merge into the symphony, creating a vibrant and ever-changing musical experience.

In this moment, I am appreciative of the relationship I have built with my piano and the world that it has opened up for me. I look down at a heard of rhinos in the thick of the forest. It's like gazing at a postcard; it reminds me of being a kid and looking at postcards my friends would bring me back from vacations my family couldn't afford. Now I was flying over one myself and it was because of my skills as a pianist.

Finding My Place

I grew up in a family of three children, and I was the middle child. Like in many other cultures and families, I truly felt the bane of being one.

My sister was loved and favoured by my father. You could say that his world revolved around her. He made sure she wanted for nothing and would always shower her with gifts and praises. In all fairness, she was a good student and also talented. She was a hard worker who excelled in everything she did as well, so I think she was deserving of the gifts, attention, and praise she received.

My brother was born with a slight hearing disability and was treated slightly different by both my parents. They were very careful with the way they treated him and did everything to protect him. Sure, he wasn't saved from the stresses of having to be excellent in his academics or the pressures of being pushed to be the best in terms of his future career. None of us were. Had my brother been born before me, where he was the middle child, he'd probably have been treated the same as me but he was saved by being the youngest child and a boy at home. Like in many other families, he was the apple of our mother's eye.

I remember when my brother was born and how things changed. Before he came along, I was close to my mother.

Even with her being strict and placing pressure on me to be this exceptional child she and my father wanted me to be, I was close to her. The day my brother came home from the hospital, that stopped being the case. My mother no longer had time for me. It wasn't the two of us against the world anymore. She was being a mother to my brother and I was being left behind. I cried a lot because I felt left out. As if I was tossed aside for a newer, shinier toy. I felt as though my parents had completely forgotten that I existed.

With my brother now in the picture, my mom struggled to manage everything in the home and my grandmother, who I still consider the best cook I've had the pleasure of eating from in all my life, would come over and cook for us after school. I found my comfort in her food. She probably thought that I didn't enjoy her food as much as I did because she would have to chase me around the house to get me to eat. I was such a busy body and couldn't sit still at home. My uncle had bought me a Game Boy and I was addicted to Pokémon. To get me to eat, my grandmother would feed me and let me play my game while she did. I also think that having her attention when she came over gave me a bit of relief from what I was going through in my little mind, so I took pleasure in our little chases around the house.

At only six years old and eating all of my grandmother's cooking, I started to gain a lot of weight. Looking back, I am sure that I used food to suit my needs emotionally. To fill the void that my mother wasn't filling anymore.

The lack of attention that I was given by my parents got even worse when they bought a terrace house and we moved out of our apartment in 2002. At the time, it was seen as a big move and gave my parents better status in the community. They couldn't afford the house but they bought it anyway. Buying this house was seen as a big upgrade and that's what mattered to them. This signified that they were moving up to a higher status class. In Singapore, having a house is a huge deal. With the new house, I rarely saw my parents. My father was still only coming home twice per week and my mother was working really hard, being away from home most days. I felt very alone. I was ten at the time when we moved in and for the next three years, things only worsened in terms of my loneliness.

With my mother now working long hours most days of the week to cover the cost of our new life, my grandmother started coming over more often to look after us. Although I missed my mother terribly, I loved having my grandmother there for the few hours she would be with us after school. She was kind to me. She never ridiculed me or made me feel left out. Even with the fact that we couldn't understand each other. See, my grandmother is Chinese and didn't speak a word of English. She speaks Hokkien, which is Chinese dialect that I didn't understand a word of. Most of the time when she spoke to me, I didn't know what she was saying and vice versa. We got along, as far as I know, nevertheless.

As we got older, my grandmother stopped coming around as often. My loneliness persisted at home, but things were getting better at secondary school. I met this girl through being in the band at school—let's call her Monica. I became very emotionally attached to her very quickly because I was so lonely. We became extremely close and would talk on the phone for long periods every single day after school and on the weekends. It was the first ever relationship that I was having with a girl.

In a very traditional Chinese family, my parents spoke badly broken English. At school, we were taught in English, so my parents couldn't really partake in my learning. They only cared about me getting good grades and being at the top of my class. They couldn't help me improve my grades like some parents would be able to. Even at the age of thirteen, I couldn't speak English well. I didn't understand the difference between tenses or plural and singular words. It was with Monica, who I had gotten so emotionally attached to, that I started getting better at understanding and speaking English. At that age, I thought I was in love with her. I felt extremely empty at that point in my young life and she filled that gap.

Now, here is something that you must know: Being a pianist takes a lot of sacrifices. Even in secondary school when other kids were enjoying their childhood, going to the beach, hanging out with each other, and just doing normal teenage stuff, I was practising. My mother would be taking the family to dinner at a restaurant, for example, and would ask if I wanted to go but I'd say no because I needed to practise. That's still the life I live now. You don't get good at playing by just playing when you feel like it. It takes a lot of sacrifices and hard work. The people in your life constantly feel as if you're letting them down because you'll almost always choose to have another hour practising the piano than do anything else.

When the December holidays came, I spent the entire holidays practising the piano. I practised every single day without fail. I had really taken a deeper interest in the instrument and I wanted to get better at it. Throughout the entire holidays, I would go to the music library to photocopy scores and go home to practise. Every single day. It would take a lot of time to take the bus and get to the library but I wanted to learn and practise more, so I would do it with joy.

As my love for and attachment to the piano and music deepened, everything else took a back seat. Over the holidays, I barely had time for Monica. I was too busy practising, so our calls became less frequent. We went from talking on the phone every day to not talking maybe ninety percent of the time during the school break. I kind of left her out and this would be the first time in my life where I lost something so precious to me. I was very attached to her, so this was a great loss; my first great loss. When school reopened in January, Monica was openly dating someone and I think that really broke me in ways that I didn't even know were possible.

I was on the academic path in secondary school and I really didn't want to have to stay five years in school. Luckily, in Singapore, there is a second chance for us to move over to the express path, where we take an exam at the end of the second year of secondary school. Before the breakup, my grades were better than they were in primary school, so I was hoping to take the second chance exam and get on the express path. I didn't want to have to spend the extra year in secondary school. I honestly just wanted to be done with school as quickly as possible. Sadly, once again, I wasn't good enough to get on the express path. I was doing better academically but not as good as I could have been doing because I was preoccupied with Monica and the piano.

Not getting on the express path and losing Monica all in a short span of time, my heart broke and my confidence took a great hit. I felt useless. As the weeks went by, I got more and more depressed. I felt so betrayed by Monica dating a boy who I didn't get along with. Life became extremely bitter. Although I hated it, school had become my escape from what I was going through at home for those first two years of secondary school. Having Monica there helped a lot and now she was gone. Now there was no point in going to school at all.

The cycle of not wanting to be at home or at school resurfaced with a vengeance. Again, I would have to go home with my report card to be scolded by my parents. To be at school even though I didn't want to be there. Around this time, I started getting sick almost every month, if not every two weeks. Life had turned to shit after the breakup. I was never really able to trust anyone that way again. I treasured her. Although we were so young, I thought I'd marry her one day and we'd have kids and be a happy family—not like my family; we'd truly be happy. I wouldn't put so much pressure on our kids and I'd make all of them feel loved and wanted. I wouldn't compare them. I had my entire life with Monica all planned out. She meant so much to me and I lost her. All my future plans involved her. I promised myself that I would never put myself in a position to be able to experience those horrible feelings again.

My health got bad after Monica left and I started taking quite a lot of days off school because I was unwell. I became extremely fragile and vulnerable to viruses, developing a cough that has been with me for more than half of my life. It was only recently after the age of twenty-eight that I started to feel better as far as my health goes. Significantly, I realised then that it really didn't have anything to do with my physical health; it was more to do with my mental and emotional health. Feeling like you're not enough will do that to you.

Imagine being told constantly that you'll never live up to people's expectations. That can take a lot away from your life. I felt like I was nothing and every single thing would accumulate and make me ill. I felt insufficient and as though I'd never be enough. My fingers won't get longer. I won't get taller or better looking. I can work harder to get better at playing but I can't change a lot about who I am as a human being. I even thought that I wouldn't become a pianist. For a long while in my teenage years, I thought that I'd just do well enough at school so that I can get an office job and work my ass off to get through life.

I would only realise this as I got older and decided to become a Christian, but when things fall apart in my life, God was always there to put them back together and put me on an even better path. I was in such a dark place after the breakup and having to accept that I would have to do all five years of secondary school didn't help. Then, all of a sudden, things started to align and my life began to change. It wasn't very noticeable back then, but looking back now, everything seems so clear.

I think my mother realised how sad and unwell I was. She rarely ever bought anything for my birthday but the year before, she got me to train with Mr Jean Yip, and now, when I was extremely down and in the lowest mood that I had ever been in, she bought me an iPod. It was a very expensive gift. This iPod would stay with me for many years and would become the friend I needed at the time and many years after. Then, just after the breakup with Monica, my mom bought me a MacBook and that gave me access to the Internet. This computer would later on open up my knowledge to the world. I would get access to things that I didn't know existed, connect with people through Facebook—making lifelong friends—and listen to music as YouTube came soon after. Monica had taught me English, luckily, and she was the only one I had to talk to. Now she was gone, I had to find new friends and I was able to do that with my new MacBook.

This was my very first computer. In my father's eyes, if you do not do well at school, you do not deserve anything. This was how you would get gifts and his love—something I've never had and will never be able to get in this lifetime. My sister, who was a star pupil, had three or four computers before I got my hands on my first one. I remember she left her computer in a taxi once, and just like that, my parents bought her a new one. She was very spoilt when it came to receiving gifts. In their eyes, she was deserving of everything. They provided everything for her to be successful. She had all the resources she needed to be the top student at school that she was.

I had also started teaching private piano lessons at the age of fourteen when I got my first student who was sixty-four. I wasn't a great pianist but I was good enough, and after the breakup, I started getting quite a few students, which gave me the opportunity to start saving. Technically, I didn't have the right to work at that young age but students would pay me in cash, which allowed me to make my own money.

The other upside of that year was that Sylvia Ng became my godmother and I never had to pay for piano lessons again. In exchange for receiving free lessons, I had to help out with teaching other students at the school. It was a good trade off because being my godmother, she would also give me money, which I would save. All the savings would soon come in very handy.

That same year, there was an audition held by a US based university. They'd come to Singapore to look for potential students to go to the US on a full scholarship. Though I played exceptionally well and they would have selected me for the scholarship based on my audition, I was too young. I had to either be sixteen or seventeen. I didn't get this opportunity, but I had learned a valuable lesson that would put me on a path I didn't even know I could take. A seed had been planted. I'd had a lightbulb moment: I could leave Singapore "as long as I was older." I was fifteen; I didn't have much longer before I could leave.

My whole life up to this point was to get out of secondary school; forget about wanting to be a concert pianist. By so many people's standard, I wasn't good enough and I never thought I'd ever be. I'd truly believed that the people around me, my own parents, knew best and I wouldn't become anything. I just wanted to be done with school, so I could get on with my life. However, auditioning for this American university made me realise that I could do better than get out of school; I could get out of Singapore all together. Something I'd never thought about before then.

There was a great chance that I wouldn't have to go through the rest of my life being constantly compared to my sister. I could go so far away and not have to be constantly beaten down by my father. I could leave behind the horrible feelings I had to experience having to face losing Monica every single day. I wouldn't have to ever walk past the school gate or anywhere we hung out together that constantly reminded me of her again. I wouldn't have to see Monica and her new guy anymore. I didn't have to feel bile rising in my throat threatening to make me vomit every single time I saw them together.

I didn't need school. I didn't need to be under so much pressure and be in a place where I felt no sense of self-worth. There was another option. Music was my way out of this pressure cooker. It had been my escape and it was going to take me even further. I no longer had a choice; I was going to pursue music. That was my only choice. I was desperate to get out of school and go play the piano.

Building and succeeding in my career wasn't by choice. I hated school, so I wasn't going to succeed in that way. Becoming a pianist was it for me—it was do or die. Succeed or become a total failure. I was either going to make it by playing the piano or become nothing.

The street my parents bought our new house on

CHAPTER 4

I'M SAT IN THE WOODEN pew, surrounded by the soft murmur of fellow congregants, my gaze fixed on the pulpit. The hymns have been sung, the prayers offered, and now, it's time for the sermon.

Our pastor steps forward with a solemn expression, his eyes reflecting what I imagine is the weight of the words he's about to impart. I lean forward slightly, straightening my back, anticipating the wisdom that will flow from his lips. This is part of the reason I come to church—to listen to the day's sermon and see what it has to offer on that particular day.

"Today, my dear brothers and sisters," the pastor begins, his voice resonating through the sacred space, "we gather here to reflect upon the significance of keeping one's word and the power of honesty."

I nod in agreement, my heart already attuned to the theme. Honesty has been ingrained in me from a young age, a value not to be taken lightly.

The pastor continues, "In this world, there are those who are quick to judge, who, without a moment's hesitation, question the integrity of others. They perceive dishonesty even when one has not broken a promise, leading to doubt and suspicion."

His words resonate with me, reminding me of one of the most important times in my life when I faced such scepticism, despite my genuine intentions.

"But," he continues, his voice steady, "we are called to be different. As followers of Christ, we are called to a higher standard. We must stand firm in our commitment to truth and honour our promises, even when those around us doubt us."

The congregation listens attentively, some nodding, others adding a yes here and there in understanding. I assume they are reflecting on their own experiences with trust and honesty and that I am no exception, thinking back to moments when my sincerity was questioned. Growing up in a traditional Chinese family, keeping one's word has always held a place of paramount importance.

As he delves deeper into the sermon, he touches on the importance of consistent integrity. "It's not enough to be honest on occasion," he says. "We must be people of our word every day, in every aspect of our lives. Our actions should speak louder than any doubt that may arise."

I recall different teachings during my upbringing. Including "Shǒuxìn wéi běn" (守信为本), which translates to "Integrity is fundamental." It's about the importance of keeping one's word and promises.

The pastor continues, reminding us that our actions must consistently align with our words, "To be honest means not only keeping your promises but also being forthright in your dealings with others. It means living a life of transparency and sincerity."

The congregants nod in agreement, each of us contemplating the depth of our own commitment to these values, I suppose. I remind myself of the times I have bragged and told a little white lie here and there, but my conscience defends itself saying that I have kept my word when it mattered the most. If I promise to do something, I tend to do it in the end.

Eventually, the pastor concludes his sermon with a call to action, urging us to be Christians of honesty and integrity. "Let us prove, time and time again," he says, "that our words are true, and our actions reflect the commitment we hold in our hearts to our Lord and Saviour."

Soon, the church service comes to a close and I exit the sanctuary, my mind filled with thoughts of my journey thus far. There is one memory that is consuming my thoughts, though. A memory that makes me almost emotional as my subconscious plays different memories I can almost look at like a movie. I force myself to not think of the what ifs in this moment, reminding myself that even with all the doubts, in the end, I indeed kept my word and my integrity.

Breaking Free

I ended up quitting secondary school at the age of sixteen. MacBook in hand and the idea that I could really get out of Singapore and have a chance at doing something I love, I applied to four different schools. I thought Juilliard was prestigious enough that my parents would allow me to go without too much fight given its reputation, and so I applied to their pre-college division. I also applied to the London Royal Academy of Music. The third option was based in Germany—Hochschule für Musik und Theater München. École Normale de Musique de Paris in France was my last choice. I didn't really want to go because I couldn't speak French. Not that I could speak German either.

École Normale de Musique de Paris in France was the first to reply. They thought my audition was very good and offered me a scholarship. I was only sixteen and really didn't know much about the world. I didn't understand what having the scholarship I got meant. I thought all my expenses would be covered by the school and I wouldn't have to worry about anything. However, this was only a subsidy for me studying in Paris. It wasn't a full scholarship. They covered my fees and that was it. My accommodation, food, and all other everyday expenses were to be covered by me. Well, this would become the biggest problem when I got to France.

Now, I'll tell you all about how that panned out—a sixteen year old turning up for university in Paris with nowhere to live and having to figure it out all on his own—in a later chapter. It was a long, hard road with hardships I didn't know I could endure or overcome but life is like that: When you have nothing left to do but succeed, believe me, you will.

Interestingly, I only went to Paris because they were the first ones to respond. Remember I said that I knew now through auditioning for the American university that I could leave Singapore all together? Well, this was my opportunity and whether or not I understood everything that was instore for me, I was going to grasp it with both hands, and that I did. There was no way I was going to tell them I needed to think about it or sit and wait for the other schools to get back to me. I wasn't going to take that chance. I needed to get out of Singapore.

Now, guess what? If I hadn't held on to that opportunity—both palms clasped as tight as I could hold them—I don't know if I would be who or where I am today. None of the other universities responded.

My parents weren't happy when I pitched this grand idea to them: leave traditional school and go pursue a career in music. They were totally against it and made it clear that they wouldn't support me doing this. I on the other hand was just ready to go. I made up my mind that whether or not my father kept his promise of not helping me pursue this dream by any means, I was going to Paris.

The moment I got the scholarship from École Normale, I gave up on secondary school all together. I gave up on trying to please everyone and being the best student I could be. On forcing myself to go to school every day though I hated it so much. Whatever little interest I had left all but dissipated. At long last, I received my well needed way out and I wasn't going to let the opportunity pass me by. No way.

In a strange way, I was considered the principal's pet because I kept playing the piano for all of the school's events. Although I wasn't doing well academically, I was still being allowed to play for these events. This made me somewhat invisible in secondary school. Playing the piano for the chapel, I could go around school almost like a ghost. No one would realise that I wasn't where I needed to be when I wasn't and I took advantage of this.

I remember one particular day; I was so bored and just wanted to get out of the lesson. I asked my teacher if I could go to the bathroom and he said no but I went anyway. This created havoc in the class. My classmates applauded me. I just wanted to get out of class. I left for the bathroom but never went back. That's how much I couldn't wait to just leave. I had no more patience left. For almost all of my life, I had been forced to be in this place that I didn't want to be and now I didn't have to be there. I also had to focus on my music, and this was taking valuable time away from that.

I had a few months to go before I left and I wanted to invest it wisely. I started playing the most difficult pieces, learning every single piece of Chopin's music. I began to skip school to stay at home and play. My mother would drop me off at school at around seven a.m. We would say the national pledge and sing the national anthem, every single day, and we would mark the class register to see who was present at school by around seven-thirty a.m. I came up with this grand idea that my friend could mark me as present if I wasn't. One day, my mom dropped me off, and as soon as she left, I went back home to play the piano. It worked. I didn't get caught, so I kept doing it. Eventually, my mother or my sister locked the piano with the key to stop me from playing.

I knew someone had found out that I wasn't going to school. I imagined that my mother had seen me come back home after dropping me off. Either that or the person who was ticking my name in the register at school wasn't doing it anymore. I wasn't going to suddenly start going to school again, though. I needed somewhere else to go and my best friend, Luc, was available. He was quite a major influence in my life. Luc was a fantastic pianist. He'd performed at one of the school's event, playing Beethoven's *Rage Over a Lost Penny* and I was so impressed by his performance. He was so technically skilled. In a lot of ways, he was the piano guru that you would go to as a student wanting to get better at playing or learning new things.

Luc was interesting. He didn't have a bed in his room; he only took twenty-minute naps. He lived for music. I thought I was a bad influence at this time, having quickly become an outlaw not wanting anything to do with school, but Luc was worse. He was a crazy guy. We got along so well because he also liked to brag. He'd fallen down and broken his nose doing a somersault while running. He was just showing off and had to now stay home for three whole months. This meant I had somewhere to go to every single day with the piano being locked up at home. I went to his place to practise the piano instead of going to school and it was a lot of fun.

I was ready to go to France for school. I couldn't wait, but the school year was different to ours in Singapore and I still had to finish up. I needed to be there but it seemed as though everything was pushing me to just leave Singapore. I remember two particular incidents that made me feel like Singapore wasn't the place for me by any means and I needed to get out immediately.

Not having the financial means to move abroad, I also considered studying in Singapore at the national university as they had recently started this new programme led by Thomas Hecht. One day, I walked into this music shop, trying to by some scores. I wanted to buy a score by Chopin because I had recently heard a CD by Arthur Rubinstein and I really adored him so much that I wanted to play this music. Back then, I didn't know how to pronounce Chopin and did so miserably. The person who sold me the score had this smirk on his face and looked at me as if he was superior. He asked me to pronounce the name so many times and each time, he would laugh in my face. I was very disgusted that he didn't stop to teach me how to pronounce the name right but rather laughed in my face. I felt humiliated; as if, once again, I was being looked down on like I didn't matter.

Here I was considering to stay in Singapore but this added fuel to my fire to want to leave. The thing about Singaporean boys, I was one of them, is that they didn't know how to stand up for themselves back then. They wouldn't say anything when they were being made fun of. They wouldn't fight back. This guy literally told me in my face that I was nothing more than trash and I just took it. He was very sarcastic and demeaning. I couldn't spend the rest of my life being treated like this. That is no way for anyone to live and I knew that even as a teenager.

I wanted to leave Singapore so bad that I withdrew my application from the national university not long after. I didn't want to stay in the system or the community as it was. Plus, I didn't think that I would make it there because I didn't like any other aspect of school and doubted that I would even get in. In Singapore, if you're not doing well in school, you simply wait for the computer to determine exactly what you are going to do. The same computer that would determine which division you would go into in the National Service. The computer that could decide that I spend the rest of my life working at a desk answering the phone or doing some form of job that I would spend my whole life hating.

My mind was made up, I was going to Paris and that was that. I couldn't wait to get out. I would wait for the summer to be over so that I could go off to start at École Normale in August. Well, things weren't meant to go that way. I was yet to face something else that would push me out of Singapore faster than even I wanted.

My sister was making my life a living hell as she'd always done. She'd say things like, "You're never going to get anywhere in life. You're a nobody. You're stupid." My entire life up to then, she'd beat me up for any and everything and I would suck it up. I never for once hit her back. I told you earlier; I was a stereotypical male, so I didn't think that I could or should hit girls. Then it all when to shit one night when she started to say something so nasty and I lost it. I was completely out of control. We got physical and broke almost everything in the house. My mother had to get into the fight to protect me. I still regret everything I did that night but that day was the day I decided that enough was enough. I had taken it for sixteen years and just couldn't anymore. I think this fight left a huge scar on my family. I decided to leave as soon as physically possible.

There was one hurdle to overcome first. To be able to leave Singapore before serving my time in the National Service, I needed someone to sign a bond with the government to postpone this obligation. My mother couldn't sign my bond on her own. Her income wasn't enough and my father, true to his word, wouldn't help her. In reality, he was totally against doing anything to help me if it wasn't to do with keeping me clothed, fed, and in school. I don't know why I even thought that he was going to help when he did not support my going to music school at all. Well, maybe because he was my father. Maybe I was right in thinking that he would care that I had a chance at doing something I loved. That the rest of my life would not be dictated by a computer that didn't consider my likes or dislikes.

He wasn't budging on his decision. I had no idea what we were going to do. Without the bond being paid, there was no way the government was going to allow me to leave the country. I knew I hadn't lived up to my father's academic expectations and that he didn't like me, but I was his son. I didn't expect that he would truly stand by and do nothing to help me. I was devastated. My only option was to hope that my mother would come through for me as she had done countless times before.

She did.

My mother went looking for help, asking everyone if they could assist her with my bond. When she went to ask for help from her sisters, they turned her away, telling her that I was an ungrateful, spoiled brat and that I'd never come back to serve in the National Service. I also asked all my teachers for assistance with recommendations for deferment from the National Service, but all of them refused. They thought that I could get them caught up in being blacklisted and that it would affect their careers if I did not keep my word and come back to Singapore. I am not sure why they thought so little of me, and I couldn't convince them otherwise, but I accepted that they were concerned about their own futures... Heartbroken as I was.

In the end, it was my uncle who signed the bond for me. He gave me the opportunity to leave Singapore. The opportunity to not allow what people thought of my future to materialise. He gave me the chance to do something with my life. The chance to escape the pressure cooker I was barely existing in. He gave me something my own father, although he could, never did. I am forever grateful to him. This is a debt I could never repay.

I knew it wasn't easy for my mother to go around asking everyone for help but I was so thankful for her doing this for me. As much as she didn't think that I was making the best decision, as much as she wanted me to be more studious and follow a more traditional path, she set her own feelings aside for me. I owe everything to my mother. Everything.

Now, with that problem out of the way, I soon had another one to figure out. The only way someone can leave Singapore without serving their time in the National Service is by completing a qualification that is lower than a degree. It had to be pre-college. The school I was given the scholarship to didn't have any pre-college qualifications. Hence, I had to come up with a way to defer, so I could take up the scholarship in France and get out of Singapore. Luckily, Shao Jie, a friend I'd met through a piano competition who lived in France, recommended that I apply for a tertiary French diploma, which would be below degree level. And so, I became a French student at a French language school, which was managed and run by an old Chinese lady; I only learned this detail when I arrived at the school in France. Thus, on paper, I was a French student, not a piano student. This was how I got the bond signed. The school fees for this school were very expensive. I took out a loan from the bank in Singapore to help with this.

With the bond signed and me registered to study for a diploma while in Paris, I could finally leave the country legally. I could go chase this dream I had of becoming a professional pianist. Within days after the fight at home, I packed up and did everything that I needed to do and left Singapore. I got everything together to get released by the government to leave and come back to serve in the National Service later on.

At a piano recital in Singapore in 2008

CHAPTER 5

MY PHONE BUZZES. I PAUSE what I am doing and pick it up to see who it is. I am leaving on holiday in a few days and I don't want to be bothered while I am away, so I want to ensure I get everything out of the way. I unlock my phone. It's a text from Benjamin, my best friend.

"Are you kidding me?" I let out, covering my mouth. "There's no way." I go to the kitchen. "Honey, is this your doing?" I ask my wife.

She looks at me puzzled but I know that she might very well have something to do with this. She's the one who ensures that I make time for my friends, that I maintain the friendships that are important to me. She often reminds me that there is more to life than my piano. This wouldn't be out of the norm if she was the one who's organised it.

"What?" she finally asks.

"Have you invited Benjamin and his girlfriend to come with us?"

"To come with us where?"

"To Italy," I smile at her. "Stop pretending that you don't know what I am talking about."

"Actually, I have absolutely no idea what you are talking about," she replies in Chinese.

"Oh," is all I manage to say as I look at her puzzled, unsure of whether she's telling the truth. *There is just no way.* "Hmm," I sigh and I read the message again. "Are you sure you don't have anything to do with this?"

"Congyu, I have no idea what you are talking about. I promise you."

I tap away at my phone, calling Benjamin. "When are you heading to Italy?" I ask in French as he picks up. I don't even greet him.

"In three days," he replies, also in French.

"Did you guys plan this behind my back?" I change to English now.

"Huh? What iz it?"

"We are also going to Italy in three days. Where exactly are you going?"

"To Pisa?"

"No way! We are also going to Pisa. Is this really just a coincidence."

It is. We talk some more and I am more excited about the upcoming trip. I am looking forward to the four of us spending time together.

Escapades in Paris

I boarded the plane; finally! It was the best feeling I had experienced in my life. I have had so many flights since but this will probably forever be the very best flight I have ever taken and the most memorable one. I was getting away from it all. I felt free for the first time in my life; I wouldn't have to see my father again for a very long time and that in itself was a great relief.

Something strange happened and I still don't know why, but on this flight, I felt particularly thirsty. I drank more water than I had ever drunken in any one day. Even when I landed in Paris, I was still drinking water. I had a thirst that seemed in dire need of being quenched—one that I haven't experienced since.

When I got to the airport and was being helped at the immigration desk, I got extremely nervous, though I held my composure. They took a long time to check to see whether the passport was real or not. It was as if they'd never seen a Singaporean passport before. Singapore was quite advanced at the time and our passports were electronic. Eventually, they realised it was a legitimate passport and accepted me into the country.

I was surprised that they didn't ask for an address that I'd be staying at. I gave them the address of my school and that was enough. I also told them that my cousins were waiting for me outside and they didn't look into it or anything. If they had, they would have realised that no one was waiting for me and that I had no home address yet. I was a sixteen-year-old boy travelling all alone. They took some time to get me through customs but I was soon let through without any checks done.

My first order of business was finding a place to stay. Shao Jie was back in France, so I asked him if I could stay with him for a few days until I figured things out. He wasn't too keen but he had a friend, Meng, who was from Taiwan and had space in his apartment. Shao Jie told me to go to Meng's apartment to see if he would take me in and I did.

Initially, I thought Meng was a very nice guy. He was a flutist; a fellow musician. He lived near Rue de Rome in a very small apartment, which was about twelve metres square. He agreed to let me stay with him for three hundred euros per month, which was cheap for Paris. I decided to take the offer to stay with him until I could find something on my own. There was only one bed for us to share. Everything I owned was there. I didn't have much when it came to clothes or anything like that. Most of my belongings were music scores. This was my very first home in Paris, but it wouldn't be my last.

Using my MacBook, I'd been able to make friends on Facebook. In all honesty, this isn't something I would encourage because you have no idea who you'll meet but this was how I met Benjamin who would become my best friend. The year before going to France, I played a concert and put some of the clips on Facebook and he left me a comment. We started talking a lot and started building a friendship; he was my first and only French friend on Facebook.

I had made an appointment with Benjamin to meet him at school, and after settling in at Meng's, I went. I met him in the Salle Munch, which is a nineteenth century room used for chamber music on École Normale's campus. I was very shocked at the size of the school but I was very impressed. It was a small campus with three floors and a basement with not more than 40 rooms, and of course, the famous concert hall, Salle Cortot, named after the founder of the school. It was my very first time meeting Benjamin and seeing the school. I remember the first thing Benjamin said to me was that he couldn't see my eyes because my hair was so long. Back then, I wore my hair much different than I do now. It was fashionable and I thought it made me look cool.

Benjamin was this French teenager with a very thick accent. Soon after arriving in Paris and meeting him in person, Benjamin introduced me to his friend, Li Si, who would go on to help me very much throughout my journey. I saw him as an older brother. He was Chinese and was studying for a degree in economics; however, he later quit to become a concert violinist and now he plays in quite a few different orchestras. He was one of the main friends who I could count on. He spoke Chinese, which is my mother tongue, so I always felt that if I had a problem, I could go to see him.

On meeting that first day, Benjamin and I went out for a meal. I remember this day so clearly because as we looked at the menu, we realised that we couldn't afford much. Eventually, we found a horrible tasting pizza on the menu that costed us eight euros. Neither of us had a lot of money. I had just hit Paris only hours before and had already spent three hundred euros of my two thousand Singaporean dollars, which was all I had to survive on—for the entire year. My mother was not going to be able to help me with a monthly stipend as she was still having to work hard to pay off the house and help to fund my sister's studies in the UK. As for my father, I wasn't expecting any help as he promised he wouldn't.

The money I went to Paris with would go very fast, and before I knew it, I would be on the brink of total failure in a foreign country.

I'd watched many American movies that depicted Paris as this romantic city, so I was looking forward to being there. Only to find that the streets were filthy often and the city had a stench that was horrible. By and large, the people were not nice. There was a lot of racism; they looked down on Asians and musicians, so I was double discriminated against. In France, musicians are treated with very little respect, unless they are really famous, and as an Asian, one is practically considered subhuman, so things were tough for me there.

It was July when I landed in France. The days were hot and Paris was almost a ghost town—everything was closed.

I had two months before school would start, so I spent it meeting new friends and so on. The latter included trying to get involved in music as much as possible.

I didn't have the right papers but I went to London during the summer, while waiting for school to start. That's how I spent some of the money I had taken with me to Paris. I learned through the Internet that there were some summer masterclasses being held in London. I was feeling a bit down with Paris being a ghost town and Meng always complaining, so I took a bus all the way to London. I ended up spending almost a thousand euros on this trip.

Now, there was no way I was going to be invited to London for any of these masterclasses had I said exactly who I was. I was neither a music student nor a performer during this summer. I no longer had a piano teacher. I was up against people who were in their post graduate music studies. There was no way I was going to be selected to join such a prestigious masterclass. It wasn't going to happen. Nevertheless, I had to figure out a way in, so I created this persona.

I wrote my biography and CV and said that I was a student of all the super stars like Martha Argerich. I asked them to "Please accept me in the London masterclasses. I would very much like to be part of your event as I have much to learn. I am very much eager and looking forward to participating at your event," I'd written. I also sent a CD of me playing. Within two days, I got a response from the organisers telling me that I was welcomed to attend on the basis that I was a student of Argerich. They "didn't even need to listen to my CD."

I really wanted to go play the piano and be with other musicians instead of just sitting around in Paris but I wasn't prepared to play the Liszt *Piano Sonata in B Minor*, three Chopin ballades, and Grieg's *Piano Concerto* that I was scheduled to play. I don't know what I was thinking getting into this. I was so unprepared. I played so badly on the very first day and got expelled in front of everyone. It was a knock that I couldn't take at the time. This was supposed to be my redemption, my chance at a new life where I would be treated better than I had been my whole life. Instead, I was treated like a joke, and everyone laughed at and jeered me. Things were not going as I'd hoped and it was gut wrenching.

I don't blame them for expelling me; I played horribly, but how it was done was demeaning. Since arriving in Paris, I hadn't practised the piano at all. I didn't have a piano. I was accepted to the masterclass by Norma Fisher and it was her who humiliated me in front of everyone. She was extremely annoyed. The other guy who was on the waiting list, whose place I had taken, played after me and played far better than I did. He even later became my friend.

With a lot of hard work put in, I would go on to win many piano competitions after this. However, every time after that, when I would go to play in a masterclass, I had this paranoia that I wasn't going to play well. That someone would just stop me in the middle of my performance and tell me to get out. It was damaging for me. I was only sixteen and struggling to find myself in the world.

I was treated like a big joke in London. I had bragged so much and didn't live up to anyone's expectations. Everyone thought I was eighteen because I said I was. I had created this persona for myself and I was almost so consumed by trying to live up to it. Obviously, they all knew that I wasn't a student of Argerich by my playing, but I had to go on with the lie and try to portray myself as the next big thing in the piano world.

The event refunded me the money I'd paid and allowed me to stay to watch the masterclass, which was good financially. However, this experience left a scar. Even the thought of Norma Fisher to this very day gives me nightmares. I now teach students who are also her students and I have to truly separate the thought of her constantly because it humiliated and traumatised me.

At the end of the masterclass, I took the bus back to Paris. Over the summer, I managed to get two students to teach piano lessons to and made a little bit of cash to help me live in this very expensive city. Back in Paris, I tried to avoid Meng as much as possible. He wasn't good for my mental health. He complained about everything constantly and I didn't like it. Additionally, he was very stingy. He wouldn't share anything, not even food. I mean, I didn't expect him to cook for me or anything but who cooks something with two people there and doesn't offer anything to the next person? I found that extremely strange.

Benjamin had left Paris and Li Si was preparing to go play at a competition in Bucharest. I spent most of my summer with Li Si, talking about life and our different aspirations and musical ideals in August. Li Si lived in a very nice apartment that he shared in Place Victor Hugo. The apartment was literally the entire floor and had three guest bedrooms and three main bedrooms. It was in a beautiful classical French nineteenth century building with luxurious Parisian decor. It being summer, the owner of the apartment had gone on holiday in the South of France. He knew that I didn't have much money or financial support and invited me to come stay with him in the apartment for a couple of weeks. I got to stay in one of the guest rooms. While I was there, Li Si took care of me like a little brother and I was relieved. It was a good experience with a safe place to stay, in my own room, and with a grand piano for me to start practising again. He would take me out, and he paid for all the meals when we went to very nice restaurants. Life was good.

By now you know that my bragging doesn't always work out for me. Staying in this luxurious apartment, I was foolish enough to brag about it. I had a comfortable life and I wanted to let everyone know. But this would be the start of my own version of *A Series of Unfortunate Events*.

Meng called me one day out of the blue. I hadn't been staying at his apartment at all although most of my things were still there and my rent was paid. He said that he was looking for a violin player. I knew Li Si was a very good violinist, so I gave him Li Si's number, which was the landline number to the apartment. When Meng called the number, the owners picked up the phone in the South of France because the number was connected somehow. Of course, they wanted to know how Meng got their number and Meng told them it was from me. They found out that Li Si was allowing me to stay with him and I had to leave their home immediately!

We were really having the time of our lives. With the piano being in the house, we had these parties where we would invite other music students and we would play music and have a good time. It was fun, until Meng messed up everything. I only had myself to blame, though; I shouldn't have given him that number and I shouldn't have bragged about where I was staying either.

With the owners wanting me out of their home, I ended up having to go back to Meng's. When I went back to his place, the first thing he asked me was: "How much money do you still have left."

I replied, "I'm not sure. I probably have about five or six hundred."

"You have six hundred left. Why don't you pay me that in rent for the next two months?" he said boldly.

I thought he was out of his mind. I mean, if I gave him that money for rent, I would have nothing left. I wouldn't have money for food or anything else. I didn't get exactly how crazy he was, however. The question was absurd, but finding out moments later that he had already taken the money floored me. I had left most of my belongings at his place, including my money, and he had taken all of it. Luckily for me, I caught him before he spent it and took the money back. I started looking for somewhere else to stay immediately.

Finding a place was not going to be an easy feat. I was stuck between a rock and a hard place as one would say. To have a bank account in France, you need to have a residential address, and to have a residential address, you need to have a bank account. On top of that, I was only sixteen and most banks required that one has to be eighteen. I couldn't rent accommodation legally. I knew it would be difficult to find somewhere to live given that I couldn't have a bank account but I was going to try my hardest to get somewhere else to stay.

I was sick of Meng and his shenanigans. Meng was the type of person who would invite friends over for food and then take out his calculator and divide the price of everything then get us all to pay our portion. I remember the first and only time this happened to me; I was shocked to my core. He had maybe twelve or thirteen of his friends over for noodles one day, and I was invited too. Meng made Chinese noodles and gave us all our portion. We all sat and ate together—uncomfortably—in his tiny studio apartment. When we were finished, Meng took out his calculator and added up everything, from the price of the noodle and the water he used to the cost of cooking it on his stove. He punched in all his numbers, divided it up, and asked us all to pay for the meal. I'll never forget having to fork over four euros and seventy-one cents to him for that meal. I had never seen anything like it. I was disgusted. This was the straw that broke my back. I refused to stay with him after. I decided to become more vigilant in finding somewhere else to live.

I met Wayne through a music camp in secondary school. We became friends and I introduced him to Sylvia where he'd gone on to become her student. Earlier on, before leaving for France, I had convinced him to leave Singapore and come join me in Paris on my quest to become this star concert pianist. I thought that he too could benefit from learning at École Normale. I mean, I had no idea what it would turn out to be, but I was sure we'd make something of it together.

I left ahead of Wayne because of the fight at home. However, I kept him posted on the best parts of my time in Paris and kept convincing him that it was the best place for us as artists. I couldn't wait for him to join me there. He truly believed that I was on my way to becoming a star pianist in Paris because, over the summer, I had bragged about how good things were for me there. He had no idea that I was struggling financially because I had told him that I was on a full scholarship. I didn't want to tell him that I was struggling to find an apartment because of my lack of money and the rules in Paris. I wanted him to join me because I thought having him there would make things better somehow. I didn't fully understand the severity of my situation at this point. I convinced him to come once the school year started, and he agreed.

With Wayne on his way to Paris and me wanting to get away from Meng, I got into gear and started looking for a place for us to stay. I found out that Domenic was coming to Paris on holiday. While I was in Singapore and working with

Sylvia, she'd studied there. That's where we'd met. She had a studio apartment near the airport in La Croix de Berny. I met up with her and asked if I could stay in her apartment and she offered to let me rent it for four hundred euro per month. I didn't mind this amount because I had plans to stay with Wayne and we'd split the rent.

Domenic had two rules: "Do not make noise and disturb the neighbours and do not have any one in my apartment," she'd instructed sternly. The latter was out the window even before I agreed to take the place. I didn't want to be dishonest, but my friend was on his way to come live with me as we'd agreed and I wasn't going to leave him hanging. Little did I know, Benjamin was in the same position that I was. He didn't have a place to stay either. Now, all three of us would have to stay in this studio apartment, which was less than fifteen metres square. There was only a bunk bed, so we would have to share.

When we moved in, I decided to rent a piano for forty five or fifty euros per month, so rule number one quickly went out the window as well. With each of us putting in two hundred per month, we could afford to pay for the place and having the piano. We only had about an average of twenty euros per week to spend on food for all three of us. It was not enough to feed one person in Paris let alone three, so we had to come up with crazy ideas for meals. Benjamin did most of the cooking. I remember us running out of food and he made us pasta but there was nothing to complete the dish. It was just the boiled pasta. We didn't even have a small bit of cream to go with it. I remembered that we had jam in the fridge and went to grab it. I added a large spoon to my pasta and Wayne did the same to his. Benjamin stood there looking at us completely shocked. After we explained to him that we eat a dish consisting of pasta with marmalade in Singapore, he just looked at us deadpan and said, "Bon appetit." We really didn't enjoy some of the crazy meals we had to eat during this time, but we were all grateful for having food when we did, nonetheless.

We were also teenagers, so we made a lot of noise in the apartment. We would even have parties and invite more friends over. There was no parent around to make us do anything, so we were lazy and found it difficult to get out of bed. In the mornings, Benjamin would bang on the piano or play his violin to wake us up. We were extremely raucous. The people in the apartment building were allergic to music. As soon as they'd hear music, they would start tapping on the wall. We would quickly quiet down, but before you knew it, we'd be at it again. We told ourselves that we were just being teenage boys.

The three of us spent almost all our time together. Even when we had things to do, we would be together in the same space. I would be practising the piano, while Benjamin practised the violin, and Wayne would be cooking. All of us would get on with doing our individual task but not far out of reach of each other. Life was pretty okay for a while. We were three teenage boys living together and having the time of our lives. Of course, being teenage boys, we were also reckless without even seeing the danger. We would lie on the escalator at the metro station doing the "Superman" going down, which was crazy. For sure, I wouldn't do that now, but back then, it was so much fun.

One night, we decided to go out and ended up at a bar in the area. We were with another friend who we'd spend a lot of time socialising with. As we were in the bar dancing, *I Gotta Feeling* came blaring through the speakers, and our friend started dancing away and having the time of his life. He sang the lines aloud, "… Tonight's gonna be a good night," and danced. We joined in and were having so much fun. This guy came over and started dancing with our friend. Benjamin, Wayne, and I looked around the bar and realised just where we were. Now, here was this friend dancing and singing, having a good night, but he didn't realise that we were in a gay bar and this guy was likely hitting on him; we had to rescue him. We laughed about it all the way home and months after. It still makes me laugh when I think about it now. The three of us had so much fun living together.

When I rented the apartment from Domenic, it was my mother who signed the documents for me. The agreement was that I would not have a piano in there and I wouldn't make noise. Again, we were three teenage boys, aspiring musicians, living together. I needed to have a piano to practise if I was ever going to live out my dream of becoming a concert pianist. A piano makes noise when you play. As the bragger that I am, I would play loud enough for the neighbours to hear and note that I was getting better. I had a Sony Ericson phone with really bad image quality but I would record myself and post things on Facebook, which in itself was a stupid idea given that Domenic could see my posts. There was a silent system on the piano but even with that, we could hear the fingers on the key and the banging of the hammers when I wasn't showing off. The neighbour downstairs thought that we were jumping on the floor and was very annoyed with this.

Because Wayne and I couldn't speak French, we didn't really speak to the neighbours, so we didn't realise how annoyed they were with us. It wasn't until they signed the petition to get us out that I realised the breadth of what we had done. Of course, Domenic was on my Facebook page and had seen everything I had posted, including the photos of other people in the apartment she said only I was allowed in.

I was sitting in a Chinese hot pot restaurant with Li Si, Benjamin, and Wayne when Domenic called me and asked me to vacate her apartment. "I'm going to sue you! Come back to Singapore immediately because I am taking you to court," she'd added. When I heard those words, I was in utter shock. Like the kid that I was, I was completely lost and didn't know what to do.

Domenic flew to Paris and gave me three days to get out of her apartment. She was true to her words. She sued me and my mother for my having broken the rules that she had set in the rent agreement. When Domenic told me that we had to leave the apartment, it was the start of winter. I'd realised how she had figured out what was happening back in Paris, so I blocked her on Facebook, which she took major offence to. She said I was childish, which is understandable, and my actions angered her so much; hence, she took out the lawsuit.

Now, there was a major problem with Domenic kicking us out of her apartment. I didn't have a bank account still, so I couldn't just go out and rent an apartment; I was still only sixteen. Benjamin couldn't rent an apartment for us either and neither could Wayne. For a moment, we were just stuck not knowing what to do.

When Benjamin had introduced me to Li Si, he'd also introduced me to Cecelia who became one of my students. It turned out that she was now dating Steve in New York. She had a son by the name of Jasper. She was taking him and they were going to stay in New York for two to three months and she told me that we could stay in her apartment—all three of us. We agreed that we could stay there while she was away, for a fee, and she handed us the keys to her apartment which was near the Avenue des Champs-Elysées. This was such a nice place to be living in. The apartment was about twenty-five metres square and Cecelia was charging us pretty much the same as what we were paying at Domenic's, plus she agreed to have all three of us stay there.

I bragged a lot about where we were living. No one would believe that we were living there, so we would invite them over for parties in Cecelia's apartment. We had a good time in this apartment but the 'series of unfortunate events' was still in full effect and that wouldn't last very long. We took photos of us drinking Champagne, and again, I posted the photos on Facebook. We really enjoyed our time here. She had an electric piano in the apartment, which meant that I could practise as much as I wanted to. Life was affordable during this time and things looked like they were going to be okay...

The apartment that all three of us stayed in

One of our better meals; we have burgers to go with the noodles

Wandering around the metro station in Paris

Holding on to the conveyor belt where we would do the Superman on my way back from a competition

CHAPTER 6

SAT IN THE BACK OF the taxi, I open the Facebook app on my phone. A few notifications await my attention, but there is one with a name that I cannot believe I'm reading. Facebook must be making a mistake here. There is just no way.

A rush of emotions floods over me as the screen confirms it is the one person I never expected to see in my notifications—someone who had been absent from my life for six long years. It's as if two worlds have collided, but in a good way. I'm not sure what this means, though, because he's never shown any interest in anything I've posted on my page before, not even when we were close.

My heart races, and I decide to momentarily set aside the other notifications, my curiosity piqued. *Let me check this message first*, I think to myself.

Opening the message from this unexpected source, I read it slowly, trying to absorb its significance. He tells me that he recognizes the place in the photo, a place he knows intimately because his mother resided there. The next line brings a pang of sadness—his mother has passed away. I can't help but empathize with his loss. I cannot imagine losing my own mother. I shake the thought away. I do not even want to think it.

I find myself at a loss for words, my fingers hovering over the phone screen. After a moment, I decide to respond. I ask how he's been, and put my phone away, thinking that it might take him some time to respond. Plus, I'm simply overwhelmed with emotions. I can't check my other notifications just yet. It seems like only seconds has passed when my phone makes a sound. I know for sure it's Facebook. *Surely, it can't be him.*

Slowly, I retrieve my phone from my pocket, a million thoughts going through my mind. Deep inside, I am hoping he won't tell me he's messaged by mistake. Then my inner voice tells me that the message couldn't be for anyone else. I unlock my phone and click on the Facebook app again.

It is him.

Very quickly, we begin to converse as though not a day had passed without us in each other's lives. I'll be in Italy for a concert, and a thought crosses my mind. "Should I stop over and perform for you while I'm in Europe in a couple of weeks?" Without hesitation, he says yes. In that moment, it feels like I have found an important puzzle piece I had lost. I do not bring up the past and neither does he. For now, it remains buried beneath the surface, and the possibility of a rekindled relationship is all I care about.

Ups and Downs

ife in Paris would quickly change in ways that I never imagined. Before I can share all of that with you, however, there are some things that you will first need to better understand.

As a teenager, I didn't fully comprehend that there were different types of scholarships that school could offer to students. I thought that once you got a scholarship, everything would be paid for, from school fees to books and living expenses. I even thought that as I was going to be away from home, in a completely different country, they'd give me some pocket money as well. However, before school would open and even before I got on that plane to Paris, I would learn that this wasn't the case. I would have to come up with money to live on as only my school fees would be paid for by the scholarship. Now I had to find a way to cover all other expenses on my own. My mom wasn't in the position to help me with the amount I needed and my father wouldn't.

At the time, I was working in Sylvia's studio. I told her about my dilemma and the possibility that I wouldn't be able to go to École Normale due to financial constraints. Sylvia proposed that I stay in Singapore to learn with her exclusively—to prepare for international competitions with her instead of going to France. This would have been a good opportunity but I couldn't stay in Singapore. I felt as though I had nothing there. My mind was fully made up and I needed to get out. So, I made a counter offer—for her to invest in me so that I could pursue my dreams and go to Paris and pay her back when I 'make it,' but she refused. Another door had closed. Now I had no idea how I was going to come up with enough money to last a year.

Remember I had also signed up to pursue a language diploma in French? To pay for that, I'd taken out a bank loan in Singapore. Unfortunately, this wasn't the solution to my financial problems as I also discovered that I couldn't use this loan for anything at all outside of tuition fees. I would have to pay for everything else out of pocket.

So, I had the scholarship and the loan from the bank in Singapore. However, I couldn't use any of the monies from either for anything except for fees. No matter what needs I had, all the money had to go towards my fees. Even if I was dying of hunger, it wouldn't be there to rescue me. The money from the bank had to be transferred directly to the school and there wasn't any physical monies coming from the music school. Essentially, I was stuck in every possible way. I had to figure something out on my own or my dreams of going to Paris were completely off the table.

I had been teaching piano lessons for almost two years and had saved up as much as I could. After getting everything ready in Singapore, I had two thousand Singaporean dollars to take with me to France. That was all I had but I decided to go anyway. I knew for a fact that it wouldn't last and told myself that I would cross that bridge when I got there. Surely, there was some way that I could earn some money to help me live out the first school year in Paris. I didn't have enough money but I had hope and the will to pursue this dream. I thought I could survive on that. I couldn't give up on the idea all together. What would I have become? Becoming a badminton player wasn't an option any longer. I had pretty much given it up for my dream of becoming a pianist. There was nothing left for me in Singapore, so I was going to Paris. I'd figure things out somehow. I was in no way prepared for how things would turn out, though.

When Domenic kicked me out, I realised how vulnerable I was in terms of my living situation. At any point in time, I could end up being kicked out of wherever I called home without warning. Additionally, I was running out of money and needed to figure out how I was going to continue paying for a place to live. As I usually do, I got this grand idea. One that would really cause more problems for me than provide solutions.

Being a typical Asian child—we believe that the more lessons you get, the better you play—I decided to register at La Schola Cantorum de Paris. The bank would pay for it from the loan that I had taken out. This was my second music school to be registered in for that academic semester. It wouldn't be suspicious for the Singaporean bank that I had taken the loan from as they would understand my need to have more tuition. My plan was to register and have the bank pay the school. As a backup plan, it would serve if I was to be kicked out by Cecelia or run out of money. I assumed that

I could go to the school, tell them that I couldn't afford to pay the fees or stay in school, and ask them to give me a refund for what had been paid up to then. In the end, this turned out to be one of the worst ideas I'd ever had. It would destroy my life completely while in Paris.

The first semester of music school had started in September. Sergueï Markarov who taught at École Normale expected me to become his student because I had already played in an audition for him, performing the first movement of Rachmaninoff's *Piano Concerto No. 3*. However, Benjamin had a connection with a very famous pianist in France, Jean-Marc Luisada. He also taught at École Normale. Benjamin introduced us over the phone and Jean-Marc agreed to teach me. He then wrote to the Dean to get me into his class and would become my very first piano teacher in Paris as well as offer me some form of stability in my learning experience. Being taught by Jean-Marc was as structured as it was adventurous. His teachings went far beyond formal lessons.

The very first homework/challenge, on the first day of lesson with Jean-Marc, was to learn a Chopin Étude and a Chopin Mazurka. An audition had been scheduled in two months and every student would have to present two works by Chopin. Every student had to choose a different work so there would not be any duplicates in the program. The master chose the pieces for each student. I remember very clearly, when it was my turn, Jean Marc asked, "How many mazurkas have you played before?" My answer was, "All of them." Back in secondary school when I would skip classes, I read through Chopin's complete works. With that answer, Jean-Marc assigned me *'Tristesse' Étude No.3, Op.10* and the hardest of the 52 mazurkas, *No.3 from Op.59*.

He was a very unique person, with a very unique life. Jean-Marc had a rather intelligent dog named Boggy. He would take his dog with him and he'd never bark or behave unruly. In all the time I was around Jean-Marc, I have only ever heard the dog bark once. The dog was very intelligent and very classy. He listened to classical music, ate cheese, and drank Champagne. I even heard from my classmates that Jean-Marc would take him to concerts and leave him backstage with no problems.

Jean-Marc lived in Place des Vosges. He's traditional French and very old school. What I admired most about Jean-Marc was how he influenced the people around him effortlessly. The way he spoke and thought was inimitable; I've never met anyone who spoke like him. He is extremely imposing as a person and has this pull that would make you do what he wanted you to do without having to ask twice. His way of teaching was also distinctive. Lessons were on Tuesdays and Thursdays and each was like a show in itself. We would all have to sit and watch each other play. We weren't allowed to leave after we each finished playing. He brought us together as a group.

Jean-Marc didn't like teaching on campus. He would have lessons in his home instead. So, every Thursday after piano lessons, we would watch a movie together, then he would take us out to dinner. Our lessons with Jean-Marc would start around two-thirty p.m. or around three, then we would have cheese and Champagne or the sorts after everyone had played. Some nights, we would watch two movies after class and would go for dinner very late. Jean-Marc would pay for everything. He looked after all of us as if we were his family. He shared his music through food and movies. He thinks that you can find a lot of similarities with music and movies, and music and food alike, especially as it relates to bringing people together.

Jean-Marc would also often invite famous people to meet with his students. He seemed to want to show us the other side of life. This was how I met a lot of famous people, some of whom I didn't even know of before meeting them. Once, he invited Macha Méril, the prolific and famous French actress who was married to the film composer, Michel Legrand. Coming from Singapore, I didn't understand how famous she was when I'd met her. She ended up joining us for a couple of movie nights in his apartment. She also attended one of our class auditions where I played Beethoven's *Piano Sonata No. 23 in F minor, Op 57* (also known as the *Appassionata*).

Jean-Marc's apartment was just opposite Mauricio Pollini's. I was having a lesson once, playing Chopin's *Étude Op.10, No.3,* and things were getting really heated. The master was frustrated with me because I wasn't able to produce due to lack of practice. Benjamin was there with me. As I sat there being scolded, I see Benjamin's eyes go wide as if he'd seen a ghost. I followed his line of sight and almost fell off my chair when I saw Mauricio taking a shower in his bathroom. I had to quickly look down at the piano keys to not laugh out loud. Now, imagine seeing a famous actress or football player taking a shower just feet away from you. It was quite something.

Jean-Marc is very cultured and knows something about everything. There is very little silence to be had when you spend time with him because he is so knowledgeable that you can have all kinds of conversations with him. I remember telling him that I admire the Jewish pianist Benno Moiseiwitsch, who had played extensively in Europe and was chosen as one of David Dubal's top one hundred pianists. I grew up listening to Benno and adored his recordings so very much; especially his boldness and the way he said things that he wanted to say. In my eyes, he did whatever he wanted and didn't care what people thought of him. Jean-Marc was laughing at me as I talked about Benno. He told me a story of Benno walking onto stage with a bottle of wine. He was supposed to play Beethoven's *Piano Concerto No. 4* but fell asleep at the piano because he was so drunk. The conductor had apparently tried to wake him up but could only get him awake when the fifth piano concerto was playing. I laughed, imagining the embarrassment in the concert hall.

Jean-Marc was also a huge fan of Cortot, who had founded École Normale de Musique de Paris, and was inspired by him. It was he who first shared the story of how Cortot was boycotted by everyone because he was a Nazi collaborator with me. Prior to that, his concerts would be sold out up to five years in advance. Cortot was humorously nicknamed "James Bond" in certain circles during his lifetime. This nickname was given to him because of his exceptional skills as a pianist. Cortot's piano technique was often described as "007," suggesting that he had a license to play the piano with incredible dexterity and finesse, much like the fictional character James Bond had a "license to kill" in the espionage world. He was a vagabond of the piano. He was about improvisation and being free in his playing. He would sing along with the piano. Nobody played like him; he had his own style. People travelled from all over the world to train with him.

When he made his debut after the second world war, according to Jean-Marc, he played with the orchestra. He played the first few chords in the *Piano Concerto* by Schumann and one by one, the musicians started to leave the stage. Apparently, the orchestra had planned to boycott Cortot—to do a sit in on the stage for being a collaborator. To show up but not play with him. When they all vacated the stage and the audience began to boo him, he walked off stage. He went backstage and came back with a solo programme. He played so well that he was instantly forgiven. Of course, I don't know how true this story is but I remember it so well as Jean-Marc told it. It left a mark on me and when I was going through the most difficult of times, it was a reminder that I could one day bounce back.

I got so used to enjoy being told these stories by Jean-Marc. It was as if I was getting to know so many people I admired through him—as if that was the closest that I was ever going to get, and for me that was close enough.

With Wayne and I living together and starting school around the same time, we would do everything with each other. He would come to all my lessons; everywhere. I would even take him with me to events that Jean-Marc hosted. We both didn't speak French at the time, so he was good company for me. Wayne and I were so young and impressionable and were totally in awe of Jean-Marc. We had a good life during this period. On our own and with the little money we had, we would drink very cheap red wine. However, we'd have the best of the best when we visited with Jean-Marc.

I developed a good relationship with Jean-Marc, one that I'd hoped would last a lifetime. He took me under his wings. When he would play away, he would invite me as his page turner. He would pay for my flight, hotel, and everything. I have so many good memories of spending time with him. We even travelled quite a bit on trains. I travelled with Jean-Marc to Bordeaux, Nantes, and so many other places. He taught me how to enjoy great food through very good restaurants. My playing had improved significantly under his tutorship. Things were almost perfect, until it all came crashing down.

Assisting Jean-Marc with a lesson in his apartment at Place des Vosges. That's Boggy in the far right.

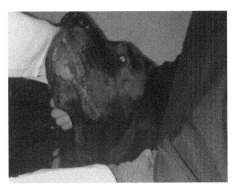

With Boggy in a French restaurant after one of our classes

At a restaurant with Jean-Marc

Wayne and I with Macha Méril

Playing Beethoven's Appassionata at a student recital in Paris with Macha Méril present

An autograph from Macha Méril

When I came to Paris in July, it was extremely hot. I didn't know there was anything to worry about in terms of the weather. I didn't know what winter was and I wasn't prepared for it. I had no form of winter clothes. We don't have this kind of weather in Singapore, so this was completely new to me. It was at the end of October when all the neighbours signed a petition to kick us out of Domenic's apartment. It was starting to get cold but not as cold as it would become in the dead of winter.

For the first few months of living in Paris, I lived on the cash that I'd taken there. I wasn't good with managing my money. My bragging extended to that aspect of my life too. If I had five euros, I would spend five euros. By the end of September, I had only five hundred euros left to survive on. By the time October came around, I realised that I would need extra clothes to get through winter. This would also contribute to my reason for applying to Schola Cantorum.

I was having my piano lessons at École Normale with Jean-Marc, which were going well. So, outside of trying to solve my financial problems, I really didn't need to have more piano lessons. Initially, I wasn't even going to attend any of the classes at Schola Cantorum. There was no way for anyone to know whether I was attending class or not because there was no marking of a register like in secondary school. All I had to do was show up for and pass my exams if at all. To me, it was a foolproof plan. My mother often supported me behind my father's back but she couldn't help me from Singapore because I didn't have a bank account. Hence, this was my only way, I thought, to get my hands on some form of money to survive. Little did I know that this decision would be the catalyst of everything truly turning sour in every aspect of my life.

By January, winter was at its peak and Paris was extremely cold. I had never been that cold in my entire life. It was freezing. I was also broke. I had very little money left, so I was not prepared for such harsh weather. Even the following winter when Paris was the coldest it had been in 100 years, I was still not prepared for that kind of weather. I still hadn't gotten used to it by then.

After being in Cecelia's apartment for about two months, I decided to take a break and go to Cambridge to visit my sister, who was there studying, in the hopes of getting some money from her. The sad thing was that I was the kid who loved to brag. Instead of letting my sister know that I was barely surviving in France, and asking for her help outright, I made it seem as though everything was going great for me there. I made it seem that I had many piano students and was doing well.

The truth was that I didn't have many students. There were times when I didn't even have enough food. I had to find different ways to make money. From time to time, I would perform in bars. Sometimes, I was paid; other times I wasn't. Once when I played, this guy came over and told me to pick anything from the menu and he would pay for it. Can you imagine the look on his face when I ordered five different things from the menu? He was with his girlfriend, so I'm almost sure that he wanted to show off but he wasn't prepared to meet the starving pianist that I was. I appreciated the offer and was going to make the best of it.

Even though he was obviously shocked, he still paid for the meal, which I was grateful for.

I played in bars and restaurants for free for a very long time before I started making money. No one knew that I wasn't earning anything from it or that I was struggling as much as I was. I bragged too much and everyone believed that what I said was true. I didn't even have enough money to go to Cambridge, so I'd gone by bus.

While visiting my sister in Cambridge, I got a text from Cecilia. It literally read, "Hi, I've decided to move back from the States. Do you mind if I put your things outside of the apartment and you can find another place to stay?" I had no idea how to respond to her. I knew she would eventually come back to Paris and need her apartment back but it was so unexpected. There was no warning; no time to find alternative accommodation. I didn't know what I was going to do. Benjamin had gone back to his home in Nevers to visit his mother. Wayne was back in Singapore for the Chinese New Year. The keys were with Benjamin.

Getting the message from Cecelia meant I had to leave London right away. I only stayed with my sister for a couple of days. She was at St John's and looked to be doing very well and I needed to get back to Paris to get everything sorted. I didn't even tell my sister what was going on. I still pretended that everything was okay. Now I was going back to Paris knowing that I didn't have a place to stay. Everything that I owned was in Cecelia's apartment and now she was threatening to leave them outside.

Arriving back in Paris, I headed straight to Cecelia's apartment. I was so relieved when I got there and saw that the lights were on. It meant that Cecelia was inside the apartment. I would rest for the night and figure out my next move in the morning. I rapped on the door and waited. I couldn't hear her coming to the door. I knocked again, and nothing. I knocked a few more times but she didn't answer the door. I stood there baffled. Why wasn't she opening the door? I had nowhere to go. I called out to let her know it was me but she didn't answer. Moments passed by and I stood outside her door in a panic, as the realisation that she was not going to let me in hit me. I just stood there for a few more minutes, staring at the door; as though, maybe if I kept staring, the door would magically open. It never did.

I patted my pockets; surely, there was some way out of this. I needed to call Benjamin. He would know what to do. I rescued my phone from my pocket. Well, I couldn't make a call. My phone needed to be topped up—it was prepaid and would cost about five euros. I only had about eighty euros to my name. That was it. Being out on the street now with no idea of what would happen next, I knew I had to be rational with spending every cent. There was a McDonald's below the apartment and they had free Wi-Fi. However, I would have to buy something there to be able to use it.

I couldn't accept the idea that I was going to sleep on the street. I couldn't. I decided to bite the bullet and go to McDonald's to buy something, so that I could use the Wi-Fi. That was a much better idea than topping up my phone to call Benjamin. I could still contact him on Facebook, which I did. I also needed a place to sleep for the night. With access to the Internet, I surfed and found this bed and breakfast that was only about fifteen euros per day and went to Gare de Lyon where it was. In my head, I kept telling myself that everything was going to be okay. I told myself that Benjamin was French and he knew the law, so once he got back, he would let Cecelia know that she couldn't just kick us out like that. But, of course, I was being naïve. We didn't have a physical contract with her. By law, we had no right being in her apartment and Benjamin let me know when he was finally back.

The bed and breakfast was horrible. It was a very cramped room with four bunk beds for eight people, and it wreaked; the place smelled awful. You could hear everyone on their phone. There was no privacy whatsoever. With the state of the place, I honestly felt as though I would rather sleep on the street. I was there because of the Internet but it was not free. Breakfast was also at an additional price. The fifteen euros was for your bed and that was it. I could only afford to stay there and pay for everything else for two nights.

Benjamin came back but the only thing that he could do was find out from Cecelia where our belongings were. Cecelia told Benjamin that she had left our stuff at her mother's place in Clamart. I was relieved that she hadn't thrown my things away but they were far away. Clamart is just outside of Paris but it was a difficult place to get to. Cynthia, her British mother, was lovely and I'd been to her home a couple of times before. She lived with her partner, Nigel, who I got along with because of our love and support for Manchester United. He watched a lot of their matches

111

and I'd watched with him when I'd visited. I was in no way looking forward to this visit to collect my clothes; not even the prospects of catching a match of my favourite team was enticing enough, but I went anyway. We needed our belongings.

I went to collect our stuff, stayed two nights with her, and headed back to Paris. Benjamin and I were left to try and find somewhere to stay. Him being French, it was much easier for him to find his way around, and he did.

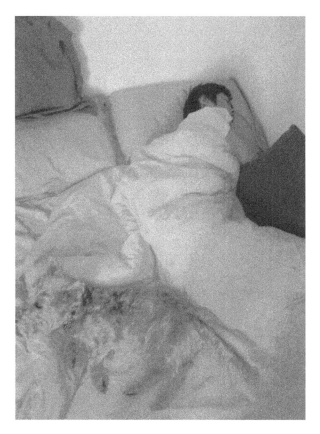

At Cynthia and Nigel's home in Clamart

In Cambridge, days before everything in Paris fell apart

CHAPTER 7

MY BROTHER AND I ALIGHT the train. One foot in front of the other, I engage in conversation with him as we make our way towards the exit. Without warning, I quickly find myself reminiscence. I know this station more than most of the passengers going about their business. I know it in ways that many of them will never get to. I smile inside at the fact. How interesting life can be.

I see the vending machine and cross my brother, coming over to the right. No one is standing there. No one is hanging around. *Why not?* I think as I reach the machine and bend over. I reach into the change holder. *Yes!* I scream internally, delighted with my treasure.

"What are you doing?" my brother asks, his eyes wide.

"Getting paid!" I reply as I open my hand to reveal the gold and silver coin. Two euro written on it; this is a grand find. He is not amused and I point out the obvious. "What is it? You're looking at me as if I have stolen from someone."

"You can't do that. It's not right."

"Come on, no one will come back for it. If I don't take it, someone else will."

"But you don't need it. Why would you even go in there to take out money as if you are desperate."

"I know I don't need it. It has nothing to do with that. The fact is that it still brings me a sense of satisfaction; hope renewed if you like."

He shrugs and I leave it at that. I am aware that he will never understand. We make our way out of the station, and as I hit the pavement, a homeless man reaches out his hand. I drop the coin in it and smile at him, knowing exactly what it means to him.

Homeless in Paris

B ack from Clamart, with no place to go, I asked Meng to let me stay with him again. However, because we hadn't parted on good terms, he was still angry with me. Meng said that his heater wasn't working and made me sleep under the window on the floor, which was freezing. I coughed the entire night and woke up unwell.

At dawn, I scratched my head for an alternate solution. I couldn't think of anyone else that I could call and ask to stay with them, and I was broke. I had no money to pay rent. I didn't even have enough left for food. Inside, I felt lost. I felt as though my entire world was coming to an end. Up to this point, I had been able to figure it out, but laying there under the window, I had no idea what my next move was going to be. I am sure that my mother wouldn't have wanted to know that I was in such a situation but I also knew that there was no point in calling home and telling her. She couldn't help from there. Getting money to me from Singapore wasn't possible and I didn't want to call and worry her.

After what seemed like hours of trying to find a solution and not being able to, I gave up trying to find a way out entirely. What I knew for sure was that I couldn't spend another night at Meng's. With nowhere else to go, I decided that I'd prefer to sleep on the street than sleep under that window again; I was left to sleep on the floor anyway and now I was coughing profusely. Another night and I might have ended up in the hospital. It would be no different from sleeping on the sidewalk.

Actually, sleeping on the sidewalk would be better. I had been in Paris for quite a while and knew that there were warmer places on the street to sleep. There are these places on the streets with huge drains covered by metal grates, where hot air comes out—you can always bank on seeing it crowded by beggars in the dead of winter trying to get warm. I told myself that I'd rather go sleep on the street and get heat from drains at nights than to stay with Meng, deal with his constant negative attitude, and his mean ways. This was worse than him charging us for a meal he'd invited us over for. He didn't care about what sleeping under the window in that cold air would do to me.

I decided it was time to get on with my day and go see what I made of it. I freshened up the best I could. I stuffed all my belongings that I had taken out back into my bag, said goodbye to Meng, and left. It was daunting. I was now officially homeless in Paris, but I imagined it would be much better than living with Meng. My only option now was to live on the streets.

First though, I had another grand idea. Bars stayed open late, so I could hang out in them and not be left out in the cold night. The first night after leaving Meng's, I went to a bar. I got a beer for four euros, sat down and opened up my MacBook, and pretended to be doing some work. I stayed there, taking quick naps and keeping warm. By four a.m., I had to leave but at least I was warm for much of the night. This was already much better than being at Meng's even though it was terrible. Now, let's not forget, I was underage, so I wasn't supposed to be in a bar. I did this quite a few times after that night, nonetheless, and was successful. As they do, most waiters and bartenders began to realise that I wasn't there for the drink. Slowly, I started being refused in bars. This was the start of homelessness for me but I was still holding out hope that when Wayne came back from Singapore, we could figure things out together.

The first night, with no bar allowing me in, I decided to take refuge among a few homeless people who were gathered around a drain not far from the bar where I'd slept the night after leaving Meng's place. They didn't even blink when I joined them. Huddled together over the drain, they were trying to get warm and they just allowed me to slot in.

I scanned the surroundings to try to find a place to sleep. There was a young boy who looked about my age wrapped up in blankets, holding out a cup. Barely anyone was passing him, but looking at him, I saw the desperation I was trying to keep hidden on the inside. He looked as though a waft of strong winds would blow him right over. My heart pounded in my chest as I wondered if I would soon end up looking like him—so malnourished and dirty. *How long has he been out here?* I mused. Suddenly, a homeless man squeezed in between me and the person on my left, pulling me from my thoughts. I looked on the other side, a girl who looked to be far younger than me was sitting with a lady I assumed to be her mother. I didn't want to go over and bother them, so I didn't consider sleeping there.

I soon felt as though I was warm enough and decided to go sit down on the sidewalk. Since standing over the drain, I hadn't seen much foot traffic on this side. My gadgets were already tucked away safely in my bag. I decided to use my bag as my pillow to keep it safe, and got into the foetal position close to the wall on the sidewalk. It wasn't a sound sleep. Every bit of movement frightened me and I'd wake up to check that my bag was still safe under my head. It was a rough night. I felt pretty worn the next day when I woke up. It was difficult to make it through the day. Soon, one night turned into two, then a few, until it became routine. I couldn't wait for Wayne to come back.

When Wayne came back to Paris, however, things did not go as I'd hoped. I had held out for so long, counting down the days, waiting for him to come back. I'd convinced myself that things would be better once he came back to Paris, and it was as if my bubble had burst when he finally got back. I hadn't told anyone I had no place to stay, including Wayne. I'd been the resourceful one in our friendship but this time, I couldn't figure things out and I needed my friend to help me. I needed him back so we could help each other. Sadly, Wayne got himself a place to stay with a family from his church and left me to figure it out on my own. I was hurt by this because I still had no place to stay. I felt as though I had treated him like a brother and he had only looked out for himself when we were faced with this problem of homelessness. I still didn't tell him or anyone else how dire my situation was. I didn't see the point in bothering anyone.

School reopened and I had to attend classes during the day again. I was different compared to the semester before.

I hadn't washed in weeks. My clothes hadn't been either. I smelled and I could tell by the way people would turn up their nose when they passed me. By then, I had long gotten used to the stench. I couldn't even tell that I smelled terrible anymore. My teeth were riddled with decay because I didn't brush them. Being homeless doesn't allow one such luxury— or at least, it didn't allow me.

It was difficult having to find a spot to sleep on the street every night and every so often, I would worry about how my mother would know if something were to happen to me. No one at school knew what was going on and I had bragged so much that they wouldn't have a clue to contact my mother if something happened. No one around me knew what I had left behind in Singapore. Before moving to Paris, and after the breakup with Monica, I lost pretty much all trust I had left. My father came home one day and forced me to give him the password to my phone. Once he got into it, he read every single conversation I'd had on it. He knew what I was telling the one person I trusted about how he made me feel. He knew things I didn't want him to know. I felt so violated; like I couldn't trust anyone.

I didn't believe that I could open up to anyone about what I was going through but I worried about my mother. I didn't want to cause her any heartache. If anything happened to me, I couldn't bear knowing the pain I'd left my mother in. It was stressful and I was beginning to feel subhuman—like my life didn't matter. I mean, how could I have been in such a situation? Where was God and why was this happening to me? I felt completely lost—forsaken.

I still had no money to rent accommodation or to pay for anything else, so I decided to give something else a try. I would literally go to school every single day to ask friends or random strangers whether I could stay with them for the night. To my surprise, it worked. Of course, some would say no right off the bat but some would allow me to stay with them for a night or two. Though the latter were few and far between. I stayed with so many different people. I stayed with a French lady, a Japanese girl, at one point a French guy, a Chinese guy, a Taiwanese guy, then another Japanese girl, and so many others.

Most of the people that I stayed with lived in very tiny apartments; I found most apartments in Paris to be extremely small—not like I was used to in Singapore or anything that I am used to now. Some of them didn't have much, yet, they would let me stay with them for a night or two. I was grateful for their help. It allowed me some reprieve and helped me to feel human. Their kindness would come at the right time, lifting my spirit when I needed it the most. Although I put on such a brave face that no one even knew I was homeless, on the inside, I was in a dark place. I felt broken.

Being offered a place for the night wasn't consistent, and so neither was the needed relief. There were days when it seemed as though all the doors were being closed to me. Sometimes it would be consecutive days. When I couldn't find anyone to take me in, I would often stay at Châtelet. It's the biggest metro station in Paris with most transfers going through there. Back then, it was undergoing a huge makeover. They were rebuilding the underground shopping centre there, so everything was a bit chaotic due to the construction. The place was messy and there were many beggars, 'gypsies,' and homeless people hanging around.

There were also a lot of pickpockets hanging around at Châtelet. I would see passers-by being pickpocketed and would try to help them. I don't like when you steal from people. If you don't have money, it's better to ask someone for something to eat than to steal from them. I've done it myself. I would rather go to a vending machine to see if someone had ran off without their change than steal from someone, which I did often. That was how I survived. No matter how desperate I got, I never saw the need to steal from someone. I would close my eyes and hope with all my might that someone had left their change in the machine. I would reach my hand in, and on the days when I found change left behind, they were the best. The vending machine was a lifeline; a way to get something to eat for that day. To this day, whenever I am in Paris, I still reach in and hope that there is change in it. It still gives me a nice feeling when I find change; knowing that somewhere out there, a homeless person might be surviving on this same tactic.

CHAPTER 8

I AM IN BUDAPEST. I love Budapest; it is my second time back this year. One of my favourite cities in Europe—charming, pleasant, and reasonably affordable. I am on a mission to record my next album in just three days. My work schedule for this album is two hours of practice each morning and three hours of recording in the afternoon. Thankfully, I have secured a decent hotel-apartment—a nice place, convenient, in a peaceful quarter right in the heart of the city and not too far from the studio. It allows me some down time as I push to get the album finished.

This is my final day in Budapest, and last night, I had the pleasure of being invited to a concert at the Liszt Academy. What a beautiful hall! It is the perfect way to end this tour. After the concert, I went out with a few musicians and got back to my apartment-hotel rather late. The night life here is brilliant! Unfortunately, I didn't get a chance to grab breakfast because I had to rush off to my two-hour practice session. My day is packed with activities, and in just over an hour, I have to be back in the studio, ready to record.

I can't go into the recording session on an empty stomach, though. I have never been a big fan of recording. It can be so unforgiving—it minimizes the artist, amplifying every slightest movement. Whether it's grinding your teeth, scratching your hands, or simply putting your shoes on the pedals, the studio picks up everything. I can't risk having the rumbling noise of my hungry tummy recorded in the middle of a delicate piece like *Images I, L. 110: III. Mouvement*. No, I can't have that. So, it's off to find some lunch.

I decide to stop at a restaurant not far from the studio and order a burger and crisps meal with a drink. As I wait, I scan through my phone, trying to catch up on emails. The restaurant isn't too busy, so there isn't much noise, and I can almost hear myself think as I start responding to urgent emails.

Seventeen minutes have passed since I've placed my order, and I hope the waiter will return with the food soon. I need enough time to eat and make it back to the studio on time. Eighteen minutes. It's taking longer than expected. I try to distract myself with emails once again. Finally, twenty-eight minutes after I've ordered, my food arrives. I have precisely thirty-four minutes left before my studio session. I had hoped to show up fifteen minutes early, like I've done the past two days, but it seems impossible now.

I consider the possibility of taking it with me, but then I remember that isn't an option—no food is allowed in the studio. And not finishing the meal? Never. I always eat every single piece of food off my plate, no matter how cheap the meal is. Even when I am in China, where food is dirt cheap, I make sure to savour every single bite; I can't waste. I know what it's like to be so hungry, having not eaten for days, that you wish for even the smallest crumb of food off someone's plate, so taking my meals for granted is not an option.

After eating for nine minutes, only two bites of burger and some crisps remain on my plate. I stare at the plate for a second, trying to decide if I can finish it. Not only am I worried about getting to the studio now, but I am also stuffed. I feel as though my belly is about to burst wide open. I stare at the food on the plate, almost as if I am witnessing a negotiation between it and my stomach, and decide that I just have to finish it.

At last, the burger has been devoured. I chew on a mouthful of crisps, waiting to put the very last two in my mouth. *Only a tiny bit more,* I encourage myself. *There we go.*

My plate is clean, and I wash everything down with my orange juice. I had already paid the bill mid-meal. Now, I rush off to the studio, feeling too full but pleased with myself.

Food is a Need

Having been homeless on the streets, having to beg to get through the day, I would say that there are three different types of beggars. There are those who are not really beggars; it's a profession and they do it to make money. Some of whom make more money than those who work in an office. They are so good at what they do that they can swindle money from anyone effortlessly. I call it being a con. To be in this group, you needed to be able to speak French. Now, I didn't speak French well and I didn't know how to swindle anyone out of anything. I could spin a story for sure, but with what I knew. Like I did to get into that master class in London. What was I going to say to someone on the street; that I was Argerich's long lost son and I was trying to get money for my plane fare home? Not only would they not believe a word of it but they probably wouldn't know who that was. Worst case scenario, they wouldn't understand a word I was saying because of my accent. Given my accent, French people found it hard to understand me, and given theirs, I also found it difficult to understand them.

As for the second type of beggars, they are the genuine ones. They need your help but they know that whether or not you can help them, they still have a place to stay. Spending the night on the sidewalk isn't the end of the world for them.

They go out to beg for money to be able to get through the day or week. Enough that they can at least eat. Then the last group are those who don't want your help. They are just beggars or rather homeless, which they accept. Even if you give them money, they will just buy another bottle of beer and carry on. They don't want to get out of the situation that they are in. Some of them think that there is nothing left for them in life. They will stay on the streets for the rest of their lives and that's their choice.

I met so many beggars on the streets of Paris because I was just like many of them. I needed a way to live, to be able to buy food, and I needed a place to stay. I stayed on the streets for almost five months. In my opinion, you can't remain a beggar for a long time. I wouldn't say you can do more than a year and really come back from it. It's too cold; far too cold. Not only that, but it also takes a lot from you, including your dignity. It eats at your body. The hunger is one thing but not being able to practise basic hygiene also take its toll. I have scars all over my body that will never go away. So many fillings in my mouth from dentists trying to save what was left of my teeth. My body will forever bear the marks, the reminder of what I went through.

Many of the beggars I met on the street were real beggars. They were from the second group and so was I. I needed help, a place to stay, a warm meal, but whether or not I had any of that, I was going to have to try to survive anyway. At the end of each day, if all else failed, I could sleep on a sidewalk somewhere.

For me, becoming a beggar on the streets took more than the courage that it demanded. First, I had to forget about my dignity and pride. I had to make up my mind that I was going to set aside all of that to ask for food; going hungry for days was just too hard. There were times when I would feel so hungry, I'd struggle to get around. I didn't have enough energy to sustain me. Thinking back in this very moment, I do think that God does special things for beggars, actually. I mean, I lost weight very fast while homeless but I never got to the point where I was too ill to keep going. Essentially, I'd have likely been classified as starving if I wasn't homeless and would have to get help from a doctor at least for a few months to get back to what is considered healthy. Yet, I didn't starve to death. I was being sustained somehow. No matter how bad it got, it never got to the point that hunger killed me.

Now, being from the second group of beggars, I had to find other ways to be creative if I was going to survive. I couldn't speak French, so I had to pretend to be a mute. I pretended that I couldn't hear people when they spoke to me and would only move my hands when I asked for food. The hardest part of begging wasn't asking people for food over and over again. It was that feeling that you would get when someone looked you dead in the eyes and said no. As if you weren't human enough for them to care. I mean, you don't always have money to help anyone but to be able to and refuse is hard to take in. It's like people who walk past the homeless with leftovers from their meals and throw it into a bin within a few steps. I had so many days when I had no money for food whatsoever, days when the vending machines weren't too kind, and I was so hungry that even a small bite would have made a huge difference.

As a teenager, being homeless in Paris, I saw a lot that most kids my age wouldn't ever see in their lifetime. I've seen someone die on the train tracks. I have been sworn at and told to "go back to China" in response to asking for food, something that we all need and so many of us waste. I have witnessed drunken people beating other people almost to death. If you can imagine the worst image of a human being, I have seen it. I have also seen the best. I've met homeless people who had only so much but still helped each other by sharing the little they had. Homeless people that looked out for me like I was their family.

With no money—not a penny to my name—and not wanting to spend forever being homeless, I thought about finding a way to get work. There was this bar in Montmatre, which I remembered very clearly. The walls were painted in red. During the good times, before everything fell apart, I walked around this bar and observed different piano players coming in to play. Some were good at playing jazz, others were just bad. I didn't know how to play jazz or how to improvise that well. However, being homeless and desperate, I'd go in and listen to them for hours, hoping to learn to play jazz.

In time, I got to the point where I thought I could play jazz well enough. I got the idea to walk around and see if someone would give me work. Pianists don't usually get a salary; they get an au chapeau (people put what they want and can 'in a hat') or a whatever amount they agree with the bar. I didn't expect much, but I hoped I could make enough to at least eat.

I went to the bar in Montmatre and met José the owner. He was sitting behind the bar; it was still quiet and I went over to him.

"Hi, I've come into your bar a few times and I see that you hire pianists. Do you have space for one more?"

He seemed to be looking at something in front of him under the bar, something I couldn't see. He didn't look up. "What can you play?" he asked.

"Everything."

He looked up at me then—his eyes almost piercing—before replying, "Well, the only thing I can pay you with is beer. I can't afford another pianist."

A beer wasn't going to get me far but I wasn't one to pass up any form of opportunity to play the piano. After thinking for a moment, I thought it would give me the chance to practise my jazz playing and see how the audience liked it. You know, see if my plan was even feasible. I shook hands with José, agreeing to play for a beer at the end of the night. I imagined that he would hear me play, see how good I was and decide to pay me cash afterwards. Afterall, I was much better than some of the pianists he'd had playing in there some nights. I had no doubt that this would turn into a paid gig soon…

Boy was I wrong.

That same night, I played in the bar. I had my beer as promised and everything turned to shit only moments after, when José looked at me and said, "So, you'll show up to play here every day and this was your first and last beer on the house. I don't allow underage drinking in my bar." My eyes went wide with horror. "Now, don't think that you can do one and don't show up tomorrow or the night after, because I'll report you and have the police lock you up for underage drinking."

I didn't have words to reply to him verbally after his threat. All I could see in my mind's eye was myself in handcuffs being hauled off to jail and I couldn't have that. Not even the promise of a roof over my head for the night was appealing enough. I was terrified. I nodded, agreeing that I would be showing up to play for him for absolutely nothing, and I did. I didn't tell anyone what was happening with José. I thought that I would be in trouble. Night after night, I showed up and played, often reminded by José that if I didn't show up to play, he would be calling the police on me for drinking in his bar. I was so young and naïve; I had no idea that this was something he'd get into trouble for too, so there was no way he'd call the police. Had I known, I probably would have stood my ground to ensure I got some money, at least enough to buy food, for playing for him. I was in dire need of that food but now still had to resort to begging on the streets of Paris because José refused to treat me like a human being.

CHAPTER 9

I AM DRIVING THE CAR. On the radio, *Adagio*, a very sad piece fit for funerals by Barber, is playing. Many people know this piece. It is often referred to as the saddest piece of music in the world because it does often consume listeners with gloom. It is consuming me in this very moment.

"Seems it's going to take us a while to get back. Look up ahead," I hear my companion in the passenger seat say.

I shake my head, pulling away from the music to make sense of what she's just said. I can't. "What do you mean? What is it?" I ask.

"The traffic. We'll soon be sitting in it like everyone else."

"Traffic?"

"Huh? Can't you see that all the cars are coming to a halt up there? All the cars are braking up ahead because of the traffic. Don't you see that everyone's brake lights are on?"

"I don't know what you mean." I can tell that the rare lights of the cars are on but I can't quite tell what colour they are. Some cars are travelling at a slower pace. I can agree to that. Maybe I am looking at the wrong spot.

"Do you mean up there?"

"Yes, all the way up there. Congyu, can't you see?" She looks at me completely baffled. So am I.

I blink my eyes a few times in quick succession but I know that it will take some time for the colours to show up as they really are. I am not colour blind. I turn off the radio. That should help. I bring the window down and refocus my attention on every other sound I can hear around me. That should help.

No More Music

This was my seventeenth night playing in José's bar for FREE. I was starving. So much so that I was in pain. My belly was aching; it was as if something was chewing at my stomach walls. This was intense pain that I hadn't felt before. Pain that I wished I could have numbed myself to, but I couldn't. I was also still having this throbbing headache that was refusing to give me a break. I hadn't eaten a proper meal in three days. The hunger was unbearable. I desperately needed to eat.

I turned up to play that night wishing that I could just go lie down somewhere instead. I didn't feel like playing the piano. I just wanted the pain to stop. I wanted to feel better. Unfortunately, I didn't have a choice. I didn't want to go to jail. I played two pieces then I found myself struggling to see. My vision was blurry. I knew it was the hunger. I couldn't bear it anymore. As scared as I was of José, I went and asked him for five euros to buy myself something to eat. I made sure to tell him that I knew he wasn't going to pay me to play but asked whether he could just give me five euros for food. José looked at me and laughed. When he was done, he told me to go finish my set, telling me that he would call the police if I didn't finish for the night. I couldn't believe him. I couldn't believe what was happening to me.

Reluctantly, I went back over to the piano, sat down, and started playing. I used all the strength I had left and finished for the night. I left the bar and walked back to Châtelet. I just wanted to lie down.

I crossed the street and made my way past the group of beggars huddled on the corner. I didn't have the strength to greet anyone. I didn't want to either. Not tonight.

"Hey piano boy, wait up!"

I didn't stop. I was not in the mood. I just needed to find a place to rest and call it a night. She wouldn't let me do that though. She wasn't that girl. She jogged up next to me.

"What's with the long face?"

I didn't answer her. I just really wanted some time alone. I was so afraid that if I opened my mouth, I would just fall apart. I didn't want anyone to see me in that state.

"Come on. What's wrong?"

I knew she wouldn't stop if I didn't answer her, so I finally did, "Nothing."

"Nope, that's not a 'nothing' look. You can talk to me."

"Come on... I'm not in the mood tonight, Delphine."

"Did I do something?" Her voice turned to a sombre tone.

I turned to face her immediately, "No, not at all. It's not you. I promise."

"What is it then? I have never seen you like this."

"I'm fine," I said, hoping that she'll give it a rest.

She didn't. "If you were fine, you wouldn't be walking around with such a long face. Such a sad one at that. I mean, you can keep telling yourself that you are fine but you and I both know that's not the truth. It will help you feel better if–"

"I'm starving! Every single part of my body aches. Every single part! I have had enough. I can't bear this anymore. I can't. And to make matters worse, I can't hear the music! I can't hear it. I don't see the colours anymore. I don't see anything. Everything is grey. Nothing makes sense anymore. I don't even know what I am doing here. I should just admit that I couldn't do it. That I can't do it. That everyone was right all along and I won't achieve anything in my life. The music is gone, Delphine. It's abandoned me." I slumped to my knees, leaning against the wall. I wept.

"I have no idea what I am going to do," I confessed in a murmur. In that moment, I felt completely hopeless. Lost. Confused.

Delphine squatted next to me, rubbing my back. We don't know much about each other. She only knows that I go to Schola to practice the piano when I can and I know that she's originally from Paris, though she speaks perfect English.

"It's going to be okay, my friend. It's going to be okay."

"It won't be okay," I shrugged. "Nothing will be okay. I can't keep fooling myself. That's all I am doing anyway. No one else–"

"Come on, let's get some food into you. I have half of a sandwich saved from today. That will help you think clearly. You just need some food in you. That's all," she told me, pulling me up.

"I don't know what to do," I sobbed. "I just feel hopeless."

"Yup, that's the hunger talking. That's not you. Congyu knows that this won't last forever. Tomorrow will be a much better day. I promise it will be."

I wanted to tell her that it wouldn't be but I was too scared to even utter it. If it wasn't better tomorrow, I had no idea what I'd do. I was completely overwhelmed and feeling hopeless and tomorrow night, I had to show up to play at José's bar again. If I didn't have any hope at all, I'd have nothing. Absolutely nothing. That would have only tipped the bucket. Though I didn't quite believe it, I didn't counter.

Delphine gave me the rest of her sandwich and I gobbled it down in only a few seconds. I barely chewed.

"Thank you," I said as the last of it disappeared.

"We look after each other, right?"

"Yeah, we do," I agreed through sobs. Thank you."

For a moment, we just stood there not saying anything to each other. She stared at her feet as she fidgeted with her hands. "What do you mean by not hearing the music? Do you think you're going deaf?" she asked eventually.

I smiled at that. Heartbreaking as the reality was, her assumption was even worse. I was immediately thankful that I wasn't losing my hearing. If I couldn't hear, I would sure not have been able to keep going. I knew I wouldn't.

"No, my hearing is fine. It's just," I paused, wondering if she would understand, "I feel completely lost, Delphine. I can't feel the music. Being forced to… I–I… It's just not the way it used to be. I used to be able to feel all the emotions in a piece and I don't seem to have that anymore. I can't connect with it and it worries me. The keys don't feel the same. Sometimes, I can't even see them."

"What does that mean for your music? Will you–"

I didn't want to even give that idea a thought. As much as I felt hopeless, I didn't want someone else to suggest that I give up. That would have killed all the fight I had left. "I don't know. I just need to try to get through tonight. Hopefully, tomorrow will be a better day like you said. Maybe, I will feel better then."

"It will be and you will. It's not as bad as it seems. I mean, look around," she opened her arms wide and spun around, "you have all of us. Well, except for Mr Don't Touch My Bottle over there. And I'm sure he would give you food, just not a sip of his whisky."

We burst into laughter.

"We should go get some sleep."

"Yeah, we should. I'll be here tomorrow. Don't get stuck in your head now."

"You don't either. See you tomorrow."

CHAPTER 10

I AM ON HOLIDAY IN Paris with Jeremy. It's his first time in France and I want to show him around town today—first thing on our agenda for this trip—but first I need to get a few work things out of the way. We should leave in an hour or so.

In the meantime, let me tell you who Jeremy is to me. I met Jeremy when I was just seven years old, struggling to find my place in my family. He, on the other hand, was thirteen, straddling the line between adolescence and the brink of adulthood. Our worlds collided in a most unexpected place—Gold Coast, Australia—where both our families were on a Free & Easy vacation.

We met at the swimming pool. Jeremy's father approached my mother and struck up a conversation in awe that both our families were from Singapore holidaying at the very same hotel all the way in Australia. A quick connection was formed even between Jeremy and me. We continued to meet at the swimming pool, and upon returning Singapore, I found myself yearning for that newfound friendship. I told you earlier how lonely I was around this time in my life. Even though Jeremey was so much older than me, I wanted his attention. I wanted brotherhood from him.

I was too young to have a mobile phone, so I relied on using our landline. I begged my mother to reach out to Jeremy's mother so that I could reconnect with him. The yearning was inexplicable, but I missed him dearly. It was as if he had become a part of my world almost instantly. He was an immediate big brother, taking my calls and talking to me over the phone day after day. I liked having him in my life and appreciated that he'd make time for me.

Perhaps the age gap was a factor, or maybe it was the whirlwind of growing up, but for a while, we lost touch. I missed him, though. The years rolled on, and I entered my teenage years, now armed with a mobile phone. At thirteen, I decided it was time to find Jeremy again. I rung him and although he was nineteen by now, he welcomed the rekindling of our friendship. He had a cell phone too, and we exchanged numbers. Despite the years that separated us, he embraced me like a younger brother, making time for me. After my mother locked the piano away, I would spend some of my days away from school with Jeremy. I was often either with Luc or Jeremy, who showered me with gifts, pocket money, and precious moments. We indulged in swimming, squash, basketball, and more. Jeremy never chastised me for my truancy. Instead, he listened to my struggles and shared in my tears, for he too was grappling with his own familial problems. In each other, we found solace, and would often cry about the hardships we were facing at home.

Jeremy had a car, so I would call him, he would tell me where to wait for him, then he'd come and pick me up. I would get breakfast and wait to eat with him—no matter how late he was. He'd often tell me to come to a particular spot at a particular time then show up late. I didn't mind, though, because I still got to spend time with him and he treated me well when we were together.

When I turned fourteen, the universe presented me with an opportunity that I couldn't ignore—a piano competition in Malaysia. My parents, deeply absorbed in their own concerns, were reluctant to provide the necessary funds for the trip. They wouldn't take me and also refused to bear the full financial burden, only giving me a portion of the money that I needed to go to the competition. It seemed as though my dream would be crushed, but when I told Jeremy, he stepped in to change my fate. Though he was serving, he didn't hesitate when I asked him to accompany me to the competition. He was in the National Service and didn't earn much, so he didn't have the money to pay for us to go to the competition. However, he understood the significance of this moment in my life, and he couldn't bear to see me miss out. Jeremy was business minded, so he devised a plan. He organized my first solo piano concert, tirelessly arranging every detail to raise the money required for going to the competition.

We charged an admission fee for the performance, and offered refreshments on sale. After covering the expenses, we had raised approximately one thousand five hundred Singaporean dollars, which would cover the trip for both of us. We went to the competition and bonded even more.

That bond was about to become much stronger, unbreakable, within hours of our return to Singapore. When we returned from Malaysia, it was just after four a.m. and Jeremy had to report back to base at six a.m. On the way there, exhaustion gripped him, causing him to fall asleep at the wheel, leading to a major car crash. The vehicle somersaulted several times before catching fire, yet miraculously, Jeremy emerged unscathed. It was a harrowing experience.

In the aftermath of the accident, Jeremy and I grew even closer. Jeremy would later tell me that after this accident, he knew for sure that he was bonded to me for life as my big brother. The ordeal seemed to have bonded us on a spiritual level.

Jeremy went above and beyond, gifting me a PSP, an expensive treasure that he held dear. His generosity was boundless. A few months before I left for Paris, Jeremy had set off to study in Australia, marking a new chapter in both our lives. Despite the physical distance, our bond remained unbroken.

When life took a tumultuous turn for me in Paris, and I found myself teetering on the precipice of despair, I reached out to Jeremy. I didn't reveal the truth of my homelessness, but I humbly asked if he could assist me with some financial support. Unfortunately, he couldn't help. I knew that he would have helped if he could—that was never a question. I later found out that he faced his own financial challenges in Australia, fully dependent on his parents for support...

My phone rings and I see it's Jeremy calling. I am about done with work, so I answer.

"Bro, what time are we going out?"

"Right now. Are you ready?" I hit send on the last email for the morning and stand up.

"Yeah. I'll meet you in your room."

"Okay. Come on, let me show you Paris."

We have lunch then head off for a walk. I want to show him everything, although I know that I won't be able to do it in one day. We are passing a piano bar when Jeremy asks, "Have you played here before?"

"Actually, I have I told him."

He sighs, "Good one or bad one?"

"The owner was actually one of the good ones. He always paid me and never threatened to do anything to me to cheat me out of my money."

"Aw, good. Otherwise..." he makes a joking fighting pose. We both laugh. "In all honesty, though, it's hard being here knowing everything you went through. I feel as if I let you down when you needed me the most. As if I failed yo–"

"Come on, bro. You didn't let me down. You didn't owe me anything. You can't keep carrying this guilt. You do so much for me as it is; you're not Super Man. You were having a hard time anyway; I understand."

"But you're my younger brother. I'm supposed to look out for you... I just feel so guilty that you went through that..."

I step in and hug Jeremy as tears well up in his eyes. I hold no hard feelings against him and wish that he would stop doing this to himself.

Rock Bottom

N ight after night, sleeping in the open air, I dreamt of a different life. A life with food in my belly, sleeping in a warm bed, playing the piano—doing what I love. When hunger pangs hit me and I couldn't focus on anything, my thoughts often drifted to those days when I lived with Wayne and Benjamin and how fun things were though we only had little. I thought about the summer with Li Si and how much I had felt like I had made it staying in that apartment. Now all I had was the unforgiving concrete beneath me and the cold Parisian streets that never seemed to offer comfort.

In the early mornings, as the city stirred to life, I'd wake up shivering, my body covered in a thin layer of dew. I'd curl up tighter, trying to conserve what little warmth remained in my clothes. The one thing was that I never wore tattered clothes like so many homeless people I hung out with. I continued to wear a suit. I never veered from always looking like a pianist ready to perform in that regard.

Finding food was a constant struggle. There were times when I went days without eating. I'd scavenge for scraps, be at the mercy of fellow homeless people like Delphine, find treasure in the vending machine, or rely on the kindness of strangers who occasionally dropped a few coins into my outstretched hand. Those coins were my lifeline, allowing me to buy a meagre meal from a nearby bakery or street vendor. In no time, I had lost a lot of weight. I didn't look like the same Singaporean teenager who'd landed in Paris months prior.

I couldn't continue with the way things were going. I needed to dig deep and figure out a way to get myself off the streets of Paris. I imagined what my mother would say if she saw me, how much it would break her heart. Although we had our problems before I left Singapore, I knew she wouldn't have wanted this for me. Yes, I was still in music school and trying my hardest to do the best I could, but how much longer could I survive this? How much longer could I be a prisoner inside myself; living these separate lives where the people who knew me thought everything was going well for me when it wasn't even close to the truth? I knew it wouldn't last much longer. At least, I wouldn't survive it if it were to continue the way it was going.

I didn't complete secondary school and here I was in a foreign country living a thousand times worse than the country I left behind. If I didn't make it, if I didn't find the strength to figure things out and finish music school, I don't know what I would have done. The easy thing would have been to give up and go home. I had a home to go back to. My parents always ensured that we had food, so there would be no more starvation. But I'd left all of it behind wanting to make something of myself, and this wasn't going to be my story; I wasn't going to be the boy who left home and went back with his tail between his legs. That wasn't going to be me. I was determined for it not to be my legacy.

I decided to take matters into my own hands. José was being cruel to me and I couldn't understand it. It pained me deeply... Until I decided to look at it from the positive side. Playing in his bar night after night gave me the opportunity to practice the piano. It allowed me to get better at playing jazz. Now I had the opportunity to look for work in other bars, so I did. When the first person said yes to paying me to play, it was as if the heavens had opened up and smiled down on me. It was only one person and it wasn't paying much, but it was something and at least I was going to be able to earn some money to start getting back on my feet. It gave me the courage to go ask more piano bar owners to play in their bar and some gave me work.

Soon, I started making a bit of pocket money from playing in different bars, so I could afford to pay about two to three hundred euros per month in rent. It wasn't a fixed income but I knew that if I worked very hard, I would get enough money for my rent. This was my chance for getting off the streets. However, given my experiences with renting from different friends, I was at a point where I had pretty much no trust left in people and didn't want to be taken for a ride if I decided to rent from or stay with someone again. Unfortunately, I still didn't have a bank account and couldn't legally rent from anyone. I needed to be careful moving forward in this regard.

I met this girl at school and asked if I could stay with her. Let's call her Sakura. I thought this would be a good idea, because we were in the same piano class, and I assumed that if something went wrong between us, our teacher could step in and help us resolve it. In essence, we couldn't get away with taking advantage of each other.

She seemed to be quite well off and took me in. Sakura was Japanese and lived in a very nice apartment and had a piano. It was difficult to communicate with her because she didn't speak French nor English. The only way to communicate with her was with hand gestures. I also learned one or two Japanese words to be able to greet her. Now, I don't know about other Japanese people but the ones I have met are very clean and neat people. They like keeping things in order. Sakura was also like this. Her apartment was very clean—everything was always in place; everything except me. I had been homeless for so long, I really stunk. I didn't wash or brush my teeth for several weeks at a time.

One day, after playing in the bar, I came home to find that Sakura had made me a bath with rose petals around the bath and everything. It looked very romantic. I remember thinking, *This is wrong. I don't want to have sex with you*. She didn't want to have sex, though. This was her way of saying that I needed to bathe and it's normal for Japanese to take lavish baths like this—I learned later. I took the bath and enjoyed it. Months later, when we had fallen out, Sakura sent me a bill for one hundred and fifty euros for heating in her apartment. When I tried to find out what it was for, you can imagine my surprise when I was told that it was for the bath *she* had made me. If she had told me before I got into it that there was a fee, let alone one hundred and fifty euros, there was no way I would have set foot into it.

I liked staying at Sakura's, nevertheless. It was a very nice place, and just like every other time that I had found a nice place to stay, I brought someone with me. This time, it was just me and Benjamin; Wayne had already found the family to stay with and things were going good for him.

One night, Sakura, Benjamin, and I were having dinner. I think I was extremely frustrated with not being able to communicate with Sakura. It had already been three weeks and words had barely passed between us. Here we were at dinner and it was so hard to communicate with her. I finally said, "Sakura, I am sure you have an alphabet of sorts in Japanese. It's the same in English; you learn the alphabet and you can learn the language. Why don't you let me teach you so that we can communicate? I can start by teaching you the alphabet song." I started singing the English alphabet.

Sakura became furious. I had no idea what she was saying but her face spoke volumes. She started going crazy, throwing her hands around and speaking in Japanese. I couldn't believe that she was reacting like this. I was literally trying to help. We were both living in a foreign country and I thought it would be great if she could communicate with the people around her, including me, since we were living together. I didn't understand her reaction and thought it was time I found somewhere to go. I had obviously overstepped and I didn't want to wait for things to get bad between us. I wasn't going to overstay my welcome and be thrown out one more time in Paris—twice was enough.

I went on my MacBook and found this place called the American Society for Students. I randomly clicked on this ad by a French lady advertising an apartment described as 'Eighteen metres square, huge space for student looking for quick rental with no contract. Available to students who do not have a bank account; you can pay me in cash.' As good as it looked, I knew from the fact that there was no contract that this was wrong. From what I had learned, you needed to sign a contract to rent accommodation and you needed to have a bank account. I was so desperate and young, so I decided to go there and see if I could rent the place anyway. When I got there, I met this lady who looked to be about in her sixties. She didn't speak English very well but it was easy to understand her.

"Hello," she greeted me and I greeted her back. "Welcome, welcome," she added as she ushered me into the apartment. "Where are you from?"

"Hello," I replied. "I'm from Singapore."

"Aww, Singapore! Beaucoup, beaucoup money! Beaucoup rich."

I smiled without saying anything in response to that. If only she knew.

As I looked around the apartment, she said, "Tiz iz going to be your place. Feel at home. It'z only going to cozt you three hundred a month. Please stay."

I handed her three hundred euros and she thanked me and said I could stay for as long as I wanted.

"Thank you for your money. Bye-bye," she said and left me standing there by myself. Talk about being direct.

Well, they often say that if it is too good to be true, then it likely is. By this time, I had very much learned this lesson, but I wasn't expecting to be conned by a woman who could be my grandmother. That eighteen metres square that she advertised was not for me. Can you imagine the horror I felt when I was woken up in the middle of the night by someone snoring? It wasn't a roommate. It was the old woman I had paid my three hundred euros to earlier that day. She never said we would be living together!

I laid in my bed extremely annoyed. She saw me as a rich Singaporean when she had just taken my very last three hundred euros and was sleeping soundly as she kept me awake in the apartment she claimed was mine. I was fuming as I laid there. I don't know how I didn't get up and end up in a fight with her. I literally laid in bed thinking how I could be sleeping soundly on a sidewalk somewhere with my three hundred euros still in my pocket. By now, I had learned where to get the best night's sleep and wasn't as scared of people passing by me during the night like my first night on the sidewalk.

As if finding out that I had rented this apartment only to be living with this old woman wasn't enough, after moving into this place, something very terrible happened to me, taking me even lower than I was. I didn't imagine that my life could get any worse than it was at the time. I had barely survived homelessness. I had seen so many things that could have broken my sane mind. I had all but starved—no, life couldn't get any worse. Only, it did.

It was during exam time at École Normale. In France, we have concours, which are more like competitions than exams. There is a jury that gives you things to do and you have to complete these tasks in order to get your diploma. In essence, you have to qualify to become a graduate. There were two rounds in this exam. The first was more like an elimination round and the second was the final that would decide if we had played well enough to get our diploma. In the first round, everyone at my level had to play *Touches Bloquées* written by the American composer, George Ligeti. Essentially, you are playing the keys that are already pushed down. The idea of this piece is to test the level of the pianist, to see how much the pianist knows his instrument. I was practising this piece with Jean-Marc.

One day, I was at Schola Cantorum practising the piano. I received a phone call from Jean-Marc, who told me, "Please never come back to see me ever again," and hung up. He was so angry. He was furious; I could tell by the way he spoke. I was essentially expelled from his class. I had no idea what I had done.

Being kicked out of Jean-Marc's class broke me. It felt like everything in my life had completely fallen apart. I had come to Paris to learn to play the piano, to get better, and to become a great pianist. Yet, here I was with no money, constantly struggling for a place to live, barely able to eat most days, and now my dream was being taken away from me. I was close to starvation and had already lost almost fifteen kilograms. I felt like everything was just falling apart. I felt like my only hope of ever becoming a pianist was gone. There would be nothing left for me after that. This was the first time in my life that my suicidal thoughts became so intense. I thought deeply about taking my own life. I didn't know what to do. The person I respected the most had just told me that he never wanted to see me again.

Jean-Marc was like a father figure to me, so I wasn't just losing my piano teacher; I was losing the good relationship that we had. I valued the time that we would spend together. I wasn't prepared to lose that. After he hung up the phone, I cried so much on hearing him say that he never wanted to see me again. It hurt so much that five years later, I was still crying over this loss. I started having a lot more health problems after this.

A day or so later, Benjamin sat me down after telling me that Jean-Marc had also called him. "We have to talk," he'd began. He went on to explain to me that Jean-Marc was not happy that I had been taking tuition at Schola Cantorum. I did not have the a-ha moment until Benjamin broke it down for me. I didn't know why this was so wrong.

Now, here's something that you need to understand: When a piano teacher takes you under their wings, especially an accomplished one, you stay under that wing. You do not stray.

This was a hard pill to swallow. I had made the mistake of a lifetime without even knowing it. The issue wasn't that I wanted to have another piano teacher. Jean-Marc was a great pianist and teacher, plus we had a beautiful relationship. However, I had paid this money to Schola Cantorum in hopes that I would be able to get a cash refund. When I found out that I couldn't have a refund, I decided to make use of it by actually going to my tuition. All that money would have been lost otherwise, so I had to make use of it.

Plus, I didn't have a place to practise and this would help. Gabriel Tacchino, who was the only student of Francis Poulenc, taught at Schola Cantorum. I thought it would be a great addition to developing my skills to learn from him as well. I innocently thought this would be a very good opportunity for me to make use of the money that was already on Schola Cantorum's account and also learn from Tacchino. I didn't for once think that it would cost me my relationship with Jean-Marc. Had I known, I would rather have lost all the money.

After our talk, Benjamin invited me to go stay with his friend, also called Benjamin, for the night. I was grateful to spend the night with him. I was glad to not be alone because I was a mess. How had things gone this bad? What was I going to do now? I couldn't go back home to Singapore. With no Jean-Marc to tutor me, what would I do about the concours? I was just a mess. I was broken. I felt nothing but emptiness. What else did I have to live for? I didn't think that I could cope or get past it.

Then Benjamin's friend killed himself soon after I stayed with him that night. This shocked me because we were both seventeen and he had a promising future. It pulled me back to reality super quickly and scared me to the depths of my core. I thought that I could be the next person to take my own life and no one would find my body. My parents didn't really know where I was. My friends didn't truly know who I was because I had bragged so much that no one knew what I was going through. I had hit rock bottom. I had nothing left to lose.

Post concert with Jeremy

With Gabriel Tacchino (1934-2023)

CHAPTER 11

AT THIS POINT IN MY life, I know that there are always ways to get through things. That we'll sometimes just have to adjust and come up with different ways and ideas. Things are not always going to go to plan and sometimes it will seem that nothing is going the way they should. When Covid-19 hit, I had a lot planned that I couldn't get to do. There were competitions that I wanted to attend but they were all cancelled for the safety and well-being of everyone.

Travel wasn't possible for the longest of times. I still wanted to play the piano and I know there were people who still wanted to listen to classical music as we eased out of lockdown measures. So, what were we going to do? We could either give up the idea of playing and listening to live music all together or find new and safe ways to do both. This was how I got to play at a few outdoor picnic style concerts, which has been a good experience overall.

The thing about this is that some of the audiences that I would usually play for would not and did not come out to these types of events. Some might have been too vulnerable to even consider being outside while we had not fully gotten rid of the virus. Others were just not into picnics. However, I gained access to a new audience. I got to play for people who did not necessarily like classical music but got to enjoy it and started liking it more after one of those concerts. So things happened as they should.

In essence, what I know now is that sometimes life just takes us on new paths because that's where we are meant to be.

At a couple of the outdoor concerts I played during Covid

A New Path

Being expelled from Jean-Marc's class, I felt lost and completely hopeless. I felt as though I had lost everything. I specifically remember struggling to understand why I was going through so much. All I wanted to do was live out my dream of becoming a pianist and everything was just a complete mess. I didn't know where to turn. I felt puzzled. Was I wrong to think that I was meant to play the piano? I was trying to live my life but I was dying inside daily. I didn't have the answers.

Out of the blue, I got a text from Wayne, saying, 'Why don't you come to church this Sunday?' I hadn't heard from him in so long. I remember thinking about the invite carefully. Why was he suddenly inviting me to church? I wasn't a Christian. I'd gone to a Christian school, so I understood to an extent what it meant to be a Christian but I never had much interest in Christianity. Actually, I had never really given it much thought. However, given where I was at the time, I didn't have anything else left to lose by spending the day in church. So, I went.

The first emotion I experienced when I went to church was comfort, which I hadn't felt in a very long time. The pastor was also from Singapore—a piece of home, which I happily welcomed. I noticed how everyone kept smiling as if they were living their best possible life. As if they had no worries whatsoever. They all knew each other; it was a small church and I quickly realised how it felt like being with a family. Strangely, I felt so at home, which I hadn't felt in a very long time.

After church, the family who Wayne was staying with invited me over for dinner. I was hesitant at first but what harm could it have done? I had nothing else to do and there was the promise of a meal. I went with them, happy that I would have something to eat. They lived quite far from the church in a neighbourhood I had never visited before. This was the much poorer side of Paris. Being around other homeless people made me realise that it was those who didn't have who often gave the most to others. I smiled inside when we entered their home because it was so true for them. It was obvious that they didn't have much but they had offered Wayne a place to stay and now they had invited me over to partake in that little too.

We sat at the table and you couldn't tell that I wasn't part of their family. They'd just welcomed me into their home and at their table. You can imagine the joy I felt when they served rice for dinner. That day was giving far more than I had bargained for. I hadn't eaten rice in such a long time. I missed home and Singaporean cuisine, which is still one of the best in the world. I longed for my grandmother's cooking, to go down to the food court and smell the aroma of spices wafting through the air as I struggle to choose one specific meal. This house smelled like home. The food looked mouthwatering and I couldn't wait to dig in.

I can still remember the first bite and how satisfying it was. Mid-way through dinner, when Xiu Lan, the mother of the house, said, "Congyu, we have a spare room, why don't you come live with us?" I thought, *Is this really happening? What is going on here?*

It took a moment to find my words. I wasn't sure what to say.

I was fed up with staying with the French lady and her constantly saying, "Beaucoup money, Singapore money." She had no idea how poor I was or what I was going through. The things she said got on my nerves and I didn't want to be around her. The strange thing was that because I had been homeless and learned to survive by staying on the street, I'd often rather choose to be there than be in a house when I wasn't comfortable. I felt more secure there in some ways. I would spend nights on the streets still living like a homeless person even though I had paid my rent and technically had a place to stay.

During this phase when I wasn't at home, the French lady took my bedsheets and washed them at the laundrette. She gave me a bill for forty euros for this, something that I hadn't asked her to do for me. This wasn't the only thing that she was charging me for. She kept finding ways to make me pay more because according to her, I was "beaucoup rich." I was not happy staying with her. The showerhead broke and she asked me to replace it, though I had never showered in that place. I hadn't stopped living the way I lived while I was homeless, so I never once showered there. There was no way that I could have broken her shower. She just wanted money out of me—money that I didn't have.

I didn't want to keep being homeless. It was extremely difficult trying to survive on the street. Xiu Lan's proposal sounded like a good idea but I was so mistrusting back then. Too much had happened to me and I didn't know who I could really depend on. Yet, a tiny voice inside said to take the leap, and I did.

"Yes, I would like that," I told her and she smiled a big smile. Taking Xiu Lan's offer was the start of my life getting back on track, although I didn't know it then. To start off, I had a family unit around me.

I'd always considered Wayne to be like a brother to me by then, so living with him again was refreshing. Xiu Lan had three boys of her own; David, Phillip, and Nicholas. When I went to stay with them, David was about sixteen, Phillip was about fourteen, and Nicholas was about seven or eight. They spoke French, and that's how I really got to learn the language—which was why I had no form of grammar when I spoke French. Nicholas was the cutest. He followed the rules of the house and never had a problem reminding all of us of them. I would open their fridge really late at night to get something to eat, he would catch me and say—in French—"You have to ask first."

I would also leave the window in my room open at nights because it helped me feel alive and safe. The air coming in made me feel as if I was sleeping outside on a sidewalk somewhere. Nicholas would also climb into my room and close the window, yelling, "Window!" which meant it needed to be closed because it was so cold. Every day, I would learn a new word or two with them and I got better at communicating in French, though I spoke like a child with my limited vocabulary.

They had an X-box and we would play *Call of Duty* together. We had a very good relationship. They made me feel like I was part of their family. It reminded me of growing up in Singapore with my own brother. We shared a room and also bonded over video games. We were competitive but playing video games remained a fun bonding experience between us, although, I must admit that I have used it once or twice in bargaining with my brother.

I had borrowed money from him and promised to give it back in a few days. Usually, I would have but I didn't have the money to pay him back at the time I promised that I would. He started arguing about it and I felt terrible that I didn't have the money to give him. However, I didn't want us to keep arguing, so I quickly coaxed him to play video games with me. Just before we sat down to play, I started bargaining, "Okay, if you win, I will double what I owe you as soon as I get some money. But if I win, then I pay you nothing." His eyes lit up as he quickly took the deal and we shook on it. My brother lost the game, so I didn't owe him anything now. He was such a good sport; he didn't argue about it. He was just happy with us playing a few more games and soon forgot that we'd been arguing. I would watch these brothers argue over games and quickly make up just the same.

Xiu Lan was a mother to me. She would offer to wash my clothes for me and shared her family's food with me. Even now, I refer to her as Mom because she treated me like her own son. The craziest thing is that this family was not rich. They lived northeast of Paris in the notorious Seine-Saint-Denis, locally referred to as the Neuf Trois (French for Ninety-Three). It is considered mainland France's most deprived neighbourhood and is ridden with violence. The crime rate is high, with gangs running the district, but they still took in two young men and helped them survive. I was constantly full of gratitude.

I quickly became accustomed to living and surviving in that area but as bad as the reputation was, I never felt unsafe. The kids grew up there and knew the neighbourhood very well. Their babysitters were like the top gang members, so I had nothing to worry about. I gained the nickname Bruce Lee because I was so thin and had long hair. We all played football together—the children of the gangsters and all of us in the neighbourhood. Even some kids who were related to some famous footballers at the time. They were really good too. For example, I played with Patrice Evra's cousin. For those who know me, they bear witness to the fact that I am very passionate about football, so being able to play filled my life with joy again in a way I didn't imagine would be possible after I had been so broken down.

Now, there was this unspoken code to follow in this neighbourhood. It was a strange thing for me to witness but everyone knew who was responsible for what. Nothing happened in that neighbourhood without someone knowing. As much as it was a bad neighbourhood, there was order. Everyone looked after each other. One day, my pastor's wife came to the neighbourhood and someone took her handbag with everything in it. Because we knew the ring leaders, we just said what had happened to her and she got everything back. Outsiders had a lot to say about this district but I felt at home. They all treated me like I was one of their own and I needed that more than anything.

Things had really started to turn around; I was seeing it in my life. I was starting to feel better inside myself. Wayne living here gave me someone to talk to and share my problems with, so life was far better than it was before his invitation to come to church. I wasn't suicidal anymore. The dark cloud was slowly lifting. I started going to church with them fulltime as a family. I had so much peace living there. They were not interested in my past or my being a musician, they were simply interested in my well-being, which was something that I needed. They just wanted me to be well and I appreciated that more than they knew.

Then there was also John who came into my life at just the right time. He was a missionary from Singapore who ended up in France and would become one of the people who helped me so much while I was living with Xiu Lan and her family. I started going to John's church with Wayne regularly. At the time, I was very discreet because I was in a very bad place and just wanted to be left alone to an extent.

When I met John, I was very new to Christianity. I found it easy to speak to John, who tried to get to know me as a person. He wanted to know what I was doing in Paris and how I was doing—the latter was very refreshing. While I stayed with Xiu Lan and her children and attended church, John helped to build my faith in Christianity. Talking with

John, I started developing my understanding of Christianity too. In Singapore, Christianity has its own place in society to the point that parents who do not care about religion at all send their children to mission school—like Catholic school, Methodist school, and so on. They do this to get their children to get a high level of knowledge. It is a status symbol that says that you are highly educated, have a good command of the English language, and so on. For me, though, it was my own way of finding my place in the world, for lack of a better way of putting it, which made me thankful that I hadn't become a Christian in Singapore. I don't think I would have had a good experience; it would likely have probably just been seen as a status symbol, which it isn't. Christianity taught me about the love of God and what comes with it. The forever companion who never leaves you nor forsake you, no matter how alone you may feel when things are at their worst.

I had a lot of conversations with John about my faith journey. He found it interesting that I was very involved physically but psychologically and spiritually, I wasn't connected. In hindsight, John finds it interesting that my faith in God grew in a country where philosophy drives enlightenment. I was immersed in an academic setting where I didn't connect either. Something was missing because I couldn't be my whole self. This was why I had to go through what I had gone through. Like I had to be stripped back/bare to become who I was meant to be. I couldn't see what was ahead of me anymore or where things were going because I needed to evolve. I was driven but I had no idea where I was traveling to. I had no idea whether I was going to die penniless like van Gogh or become a great pianist.

John and his wife encouraged me. I didn't feel like I was in competition when I was around them. There was no comparison. They just wanted to get to know me as a human being and make sure that I was okay. I felt safe to be vulnerable. Almost as if I had the chance to really be a child. I didn't have anything to prove. Every mistake throughout my life was criticized from childhood; it was refreshing that I didn't have to deal with that from them. John and I talked about life and the struggles that we both encounter in life, and I wasn't judged. It was easy to be around him and with him. He never wanted to make me into anything like him. He gave me the space to figure out what God wanted for me.

John was so shocked when I adopted him as my spiritual father but I did that because he was the kind of father I would have wanted all my life. He showed me that someone can see all of me, without any fluffs, without any bragging, and still like me. To top it all off, whereas my biological father never saw me play, John would come to my concerts to support me.

My faith started to grow. I had these weird moments where I'd be trying to cross the street and I'd say, "Oh God, please let this light turn green," and it would. Or I'd be very hungry and say, "Oh God, please feed me, I'm hungry," and someone would offer me food right then and there. It's something that I can't explain entirely but I started praying and asking God and he would provide it. I remember going to church and the pastor said, "God will never let his children starve." Inside, I thought, *Are you sure? Because I have been starving a lot.* However, in the very same breath, I prayed to God, asking him to never let me starve again.

After praying this prayer, I went to a concert by Li Si who was preparing for his final year exam. The school had given him a slot at the concert hall to have an afternoon recital. Li Si had always been kind to me. It was the first time that he had seen me in months. I stood in front of him, a skeleton of the person I was months prior. I was under forty-five kilograms, and looked like I had survived a war with no food. He was with Gu Yue. He was a student architect who had recently found a well-paid job. We had talked about life and music and had banter but I never hung out with Gu Yue because he was much older. When they saw me after Li Si's concert, they couldn't believe how much weight I had lost. I remember Li Si saying, "What happened to you? You have to eat." I didn't tell him everything but Gu Yue gave me two books of restaurant tickets, with each book having thirty tickets. Each ticket was worth seven euros fifty cent. To me, this was God answering my prayers. I wouldn't starve again. He'd provided me with at least one meal per day for two whole months and that would give me enough time to figure things out.

I decided not to give up on my dream and went to talk with the principal at École Normale, Jean Louis Mansart, about what to do with Jean-Marc not wanting to tutor me anymore. He had a stern face and a stiff voice. He had a reputation of making students cry, so I was scared of going to see him but I had no other option at this point. So, I put on a brave face and went to speak with him. I remember whilst waiting for my turn to be interviewed, I was in front of three female Korean students in tears, which made me quite nervous.

Meeting with him was not as dreadful for me, luckily. He gave me a way out. He explained things to me, saying that having a piano teacher is like having a wife; you cannot have two at the same time. Just like if you want to see other women, you have to speak with your wife first to get permission, it is the exact same with your piano teacher. You have to get their permission if you want to get tutored by someone else. It was a strange analogy but I understood exactly what he meant and it made me realise that Jean-Marc had felt completely betrayed by me. He treated me like his star student and had helped me to develop in so many different aspects of my life and I had betrayed him without even knowing. Realising this made me almost as sad as I was when he had called me that day while at Schola Cantorum.

Jean Louis Mansart gave me another piano teacher to help me finish up my preparations for the concours. Her name was Odile Catelin-Delangle. She was the wife of Claude Delangle, the very famous French saxophonist. She was a brilliant teacher in her own right. I have never met anyone in my life who was as patient as her. She was very warm. Unlike Jean-Marc who'd gone to study in England from a very early age and spoke English fluently, she didn't speak a single word of English. We communicated with hand signals and Google Translate on my Sony Ericson phone. While I learned to play the piece for my concours with Odile, I didn't have a piano at home, and the hall at Schola

Cantorum was not available after five p.m., so I carved the piano keys into a table in my rental, which I kept until I felt completely safe at Xiu Lan's, and would practise some more there. I would just tap away, memorising the sequence to play the keys in.

I went to sit the first part of the concours and passed. More than half of the students who played failed. Never before then had I played that well without practice. I wasn't prepared physically but I was prepared mentally. I had practiced inside my head and knew the music entirely. I had developed a new skill and it would help me much later in life.

The hardest part of being in Paris was over now. I was no longer living on the streets. I was being paid for playing in bars but I still didn't have much money. I heard about a piano competition happening in Berlin. The grand prize was two thousand euros. Back then, it was a lot of money. I took a bus from Paris to Berlin—it was about seventeen hours. I arrived in Berlin at eleven in the morning and played at three-thirty p.m. I played Beethoven's *Appassionata* in a one hour solo programme. This was being judged by a mixed of jurors made up of German and Russian judges, and playing a German composer's music, I won the grand prize. This was where the table started to really turn. Though it wasn't a big competition, it was the start of me getting back on track.

The money that I won helped me so much. I used it to survive as well as apply for many other competitions in Slovenia, Italy, Switzerland, and other places and was successful in many of them as well. The next thing I decided to do after winning the competition in Berlin was to get baptised. I had the realisation that my only purpose in life was to serve God with my music. I was going to die and I'd met Him again. He'd literally saved me from my own vomit. He took me up, dusted me off, and put me back in a clean place again.

Even when I would have the thoughts to kill myself or be ready to jump into moving traffic while being homeless, I would hear a voice inside telling me that I had more to live for. That my story wasn't finished yet. I would literally hear something inside telling me that I still had more to give. Here I was living the truth of that, so the only thing left for me to do was give my life to God. To serve him through the very gift that he had given me. I was desperate and lonely and God brought people into my life to pull me out of that state. Since committing my life to God, the purpose of my life changed and so did my music.

With John Lim, my spiritual father

Having dinner with John Lim on my nineteenth birthday

Waiting to see the principal at École Normale

After winning first prize at a competition in Vulaine

Before a public masterclass in Switzerland with Pierto de Maria

Semi-finalist at the piano campus in 2011

Finalist at the Chatou Piano Competition in 2011

A photoshoot I had in 2011

CHAPTER 12

I AM ALREADY SEATED; ROW three, seat c. A man sits down next to me but I don't look up. He greets me and I do the same, still not taking my eyes off what I am holding in my hand. He twists and turns as if he is uncomfortable and I shift to give him more room, hoping that I am not hogging the space too much.

I go back to practising. I am so engrossed that I don't realise that we have already taken off. Soon, the seatbelt signs are turned off. Suddenly, I hear, "What's that? All those papers, so many lines."

"They are music sheets."

"Oh, are you a music teacher?"

"Actually, I am headed to a concert that I'll be playing at."

His mouth open as his eyes grow large. He's staring at me confused. Then he asks, "So, why are you reading those? Don't you just look at it while you're playing?"

"Well, yes and no. But I'm actually practising. I want to be ready when I get there."

His eyes grow larger as he looks more puzzled. "What do you mean? You don't have a piano here."

"I'm rehearsing in my head."

"How? Do you know the keys that well?"

"Yeah, I actually do."

New Beginnings

started to find the simple joys in life again. Going to church and being around people who were there to encourage me helped me to start seeing life in new light. I had much to be thankful for.

It was still a struggle dealing with losing Jean-Marc as my teacher but I had to look on the bright side. Odile was tutoring me at École Normale and I continued on at Schola Cantorum. I reminded myself that I had learnt everything I knew from Jean-Marc before he expelled me, which I was grateful for, but I still had people to help me and needed to embrace that. There was still a lot for me to learn. With Nina, my chamber music teacher, I was learning how to listen, accommodate, and accompany other musicians. She taught me how to not be a selfish musician. I played in a duet with my friend, Benjamin, and she graded us well. To this day, Benjamin and I still play well together.

Even though I only spent a little time with him, I also learned something valuable from Aquiles Delle Vigne. He was a very famous pianist from Argentina who was based in Brussels and had watched me play in a piano competition in the conservatory in Paris. He was very impressed with my playing and invited me to visit him in Brussels to play for him privately. I wasn't very close with him but we had a very good connection; we enjoyed drinking and talking about red wine. He had a beautiful aura about him that when you stood next to him, you felt like you were a very good friend. He was probably one of the best pianist I have ever known. He was taught by Arrau, and he shared with me that he taught him that a musician must never cheat. When things get easy, it is very easy to substitute fingering or hands. You will want to add things or remove things, but play the score as it is. Stick to the score and keep the music pure. This is something that I still hold on to today.

I remained at Schola Cantorum and learned under Gabriel Tacchino. He would share a lot with me. He told me that he played in a casino in the South of France and Poulenc went to watch him play. I mean, imagine me playing for Chopin; it would be such a huge honour. He played a short piece called *Presto*. The piece is only two minutes long but he had a memory slip and forgot how to finish the piece, so he ended up playing for five minutes. He thought that he would disappoint his master so badly. However, when he saw Poulenc at the end of the piece, he said that he hadn't even realised that Gabriel had played it more than once and that he'd done a good job. This made me realise that Poulenc was not like many composers; he was easy going.

Gabriel Tacchino was quite old when I met him. I believe he was about seventy-six. He wasn't living in Paris; he was living in his home town of Cannes. He would fly to Paris to come to lessons. Every time I would play for him, I had this impression that he couldn't hear me play because there was still pressure from the flight disturbing his hearing. I thought he was more like a grandmaster than someone to be teaching students by this time. He gave me a lot of freedom and never gave me a single homework in all my studying with him. He was also a bit forgetful or slow. I would be playing and make a mistake and I would play to page seven or eight and he would be at page one or two trying to figure out what went wrong by the time I would have finished the piece. He would have forgotten what he wanted to say by then.

Gabriel said that Poulenc didn't like too much rubato. This is a term for being free, slowing down and expressing yourself. He like music to be very baroque without too much interpretation. The score must be respected. He doesn't like when pianists try to recreate pieces. I understood what he meant. It's like if Tom Cruise was to play Batman, you wouldn't see Batman as the Batman that you know. It would be more difficult to connect. He is Tom Cruise. They play their roles and it makes sense. You can play a piece but if you don't respect the score, it doesn't sound as good as it should. You can't play Chopin to make it sound like Poulenc's music. Play Chopin so people recognise the music.

When you play a note, every note goes with the keys. However, at a high note, when you're playing with emotions and full liberty, sometimes the notes on the right hand go a little bit later than the left. This sounds freeing and even romantic. The right hand is like a singer and the left hand is like the orchestra. This is how it was played in the nineteenth century. Poulenc thought that this wasn't necessary. That you should be expressive in other ways. Not like this.

Playing for Tacchino was more like a privilege to play for the master to know if you were ready for your concert or not more than it was a lesson. However, he was very famous and had very good connections and advised me to play for some of his friends who were also very influential pianists. Through Tacchino, I was able to play for the likes of Sergio Perticaroli, who was a leading pianist in his time. He had lived through the wars and had a brilliant career. He'd played all over Europe and when he met the Russian composer Aram Khachaturian, he played his own *Piano Concerto in D-flat* for him.

It was a huge privilege to meet and play for Tacchino as he's worked with many of my heroes when they were alive. Now here I was as a seventeen-year-old kid from Singapore playing for Perticaroli. I played a Beethoven sonata for him and when I finished, he said, "You're going to have a brilliant career. There is absolutely nothing that I can say to you, but we can play together." I was floored. We played together and this was my very first masterclass where the teacher played simultaneously on a second piano the entire time. I never learned anything from him but the words he said to me fuelled me and helped me to believe that I would one day become a great pianist, which was my greatest dream.

I met Éric Heidsieck through working with Tacchino. When I met Éric, it was through a public masterclass at Schola. It was a masterclass dedicated to his compositions. He wrote a book of arrangements on the theme of the French national anthem. For instance, in the style of Bach, Mozart, and Chopin. Essentially, this composition is of Éric trying to reimagine how these composers would have written the French national anthem if they were alive. So, they have different sounds.

Pianists had come from all over the world for these masterclasses. There was this guy who travelled with his piano bench all the way from Japan to the masterclass because, seemingly, this was the only bench that he could play from. His whole masterclass was about him adjusting his bench. In all honesty, I found this weird.

Now, silly me, who didn't understand French at the time, didn't understand that this masterclass was for us to play from the compositions of Heidsieck. I thought we could play anything by any of the composers I had seen on this list. I saw their names but did not make the connection. I played completely outside of Heidsieck's compositions. I played a Mazurka by Chopin. Everyone in the audience was baffled. No one understood why I had played the Mazurka; even Heidsieck was puzzled, though he liked how I played.

He said into the microphone, "Oh, please forgive us. I think today we have an intruder from Singapore, who has no idea what this masterclass is about, but let's just do this masterclass anyway." Although he was a little offended that I didn't play his composition, he wasn't angry. You could almost say that he took it on the chin—his ego wasn't bruised. This was the first time that I had played for him and I was in awe of him as a human being. He gave me his phone number and told me to call him and come visit him so we could have a drink together. I took the offer and visited him. On that visit, I learned that Charles Heidsieck was his father who had inherited the Heidsieck Champagne empire, which he sold later on. He later on became like a grandfather to me. I admired his humility and model that in my own life today.

I remember the first time I went to Éric's for a meal. There were only two sausages, one for him and one for me. I was so shocked—to me, there was nothing on the plate. I've learned that rich people don't eat a lot; they seem to rather drink their calories. He had some of the best alcohols in his house; a lot of drinks but not a lot of food. I remember sitting at his kitchen table and he said to me, "Do you know that Rubinstein sat on that chair?" then went on to tell me about so many of my idols who had sat on that very chair or in that very room. I thought, *Oh my God!* I melted onto the floor. The number of great pianists, so many of my idols, who had been in that very room where I was seated was mindboggling in the best of ways. Here I was—Congyu from Singapore; 'a nobody' at the time—sitting in this room, on the same chair where some of my idols had no doubt sat themselves.

A lot of people go on about how important expressing gratitude is: I believe them. God was always looking after me but I didn't realise it. He was moulding me when he took me through the worse of things. As I began to appreciate all the things that I was grateful for, all the lessons I was learning through people so many pianists would give anything to learn from, other parts of my life also began to align.

I never expected to find love in Paris; I was too focused on being a pianist. Then, as fate would have it, I met my now wife, Julie, in June 2011. When I met Julie the first time, she thought that I smelled awful, and I did. I had really long hair.

I wore an Elvis Presley haircut back then. I'd only wash my hair every two weeks. Xiu Lan couldn't afford to pay for enough heating, so I didn't waste. Even the water that I used to bathe would have to be saved to flush the toilet later; conservation was absolutely necessary. I didn't realise that I stank. I mean, I had been homeless for months at a time before then and wasn't able to bathe for weeks, two weeks was a step in the right direction.

Within a week of hanging out, we were talking about getting engaged. When I met her, I was only nineteen years old, but the only thing I was thinking about was continuing to have stability in my life. I wanted to be stable and to never again have to starve or go through what I had been through thus far. I even thought of getting a teaching job in a music school to be able to settle and start living a more stable and secured life. Settling down with a wife soon after figuring out all of that was a welcomed idea.

I believe that everything happens for a reason and life flows in one direction, ending up somewhere. As a child, my wife hated the piano, so she never expected to marry a pianist. That was the last thing that she would ever imagine doing. She studied in Bordeaux then in Lille. She had to do an internship and did not want to go to Paris. She begged her parents to not send her there. She thought it was dirty and crowded and she never wanted to have to live there doing her internship. However, she got her internship at a big company in Paris. It was a well-paid position as an intern and she made the move. She got an apartment located in the thirteenth arrondissement of Paris which is known as the Chinatown of Paris.

185

Julie is from a very disciplined Christian Chinese family. Her mother told her to look for a church in Paris to attend while she was there. More specifically, her mother wanted her to look for a Chinese speaking church. She had just come back from a trip in Beijing and started her search. Thus, the coincidence of her living only five hundred metres from the church I attended, and where I played the piano every Sunday, caused our paths to cross. Strangely, when she met me, she thought I was a very bad pianist. I was playing in church with a singer and things just did not go well. I hadn't been able to attend the rehearsals for the service because I had been teaching the whole week. I improvised but it didn't work out well and she could tell. Not a good first impression.

I remember that day and the first time I laid eyes on her. She had a glow about her as she went around greeting everyone. There was this beautiful light around her and she was well-spoken. I thought, *Wow, I have to get to know her.* She spoke English, French, and Chinese so well; I was very impressed with her Chinese. I finally got the chance to meet her.

I went up to her and she introduced herself immediately, "Hi, I'm from Réunion island."

I smiled and replied, "Hi, I'm from Singapore." It was a brief introduction but at least I got the chance to say hello to her and now knew she was from Réunion island, though I had no idea where that was.

After church, the young people met up as we usually did and we went to the movies. Julie joined us. Before we went to the movies, I sat playing with the PSP Jeremy had bought me years earlier and wasn't even looking at Julie when she was speaking with me. I was playing FIFA 2010. Wayne Rooney was my favourite player and I was having a good time playing my game. Julie told me later that she thought I was very childish because of this.

Initially, I wasn't interested in Julie romantically. When I first saw her, I thought that we could be really good friends. I thought I could learn from her. There is the Fête de la Musique in France, what would be translated as Music Day in English, which falls on June 21 each year. So, the group of young people from church organised a get together for all of us. This was the second time that I met her. This time, I didn't have a PSP and it was nice to see her. We talked, and she seemed to really listen to me, and we exchanged details about our lives. Like many other people before her, Julie was really shocked about what I had been through in my life. Even to this day, she thinks that my story is a fairy tale.

During this event, we had dinner and as we got to know each other, I realised that I had a romantic interest in her but I never thought that it would go far. I had a concert that was coming up that weekend. It wasn't a big event or anything but I decided to invite her. I was still a student and was playing for the end of the year auditions. I invited her to come and watch. I didn't explain exactly what I was playing at and Julie thought I was playing at some opera concert or something.

At this point in time, I was also having tutoring with my Russian teacher, Igor Lazko. He was one of the most interesting teachers I have ever worked with. He spoke with disinterest, as if he wasn't interested in conversation. However, when he played the piano or demonstrated something on the keyboard, he was such a monster. At the age of fifteen, he'd won third prize in the J.S. Bach International Piano Competition in Leipzig. He also organised quite a few events and would get us to perform as his students; this was one of those concerts. The biggest lesson he taught me was that "There is nothing more difficult in life because there is nothing more difficult than playing the piano. There's also nothing that is impossible to play on the piano. You have a brain, so every technical difficulty can be overcome. There is no such thing as being impossible." It was with him that I learned that one had to be patient and find their way, which will happen eventually. Every one of us are different and will react differently to things because we are all diverse in everything that we are. This is where I developed the mentality that every single thing is doable.

Julie agreed to come to the event and asked for time off at work. The concert was being held in the Bastille, a famous square in Paris. It was NOT at the Opéra Bastille as Julie had thought. The venue I was playing at was on the same street but was a very much smaller venue, in a very small music shop that sold instruments and flutes.

There were about thirty-five of us and I was the last to play. The room was so tiny that some people were sitting on the stairs. When I spoke to Julie later, she told me how puzzled she was that I was the very last to play. She'd sat there thinking how terrible I was that I was kept for last.

Remember, she had seen me play at church before and I was terrible on that keyboard. There were teens who were not yet very good playing at this concert as well and they'd gone ahead of me. This made Julie think it was all a big joke. She thought that I was a French major, that I was simply in Paris to learn French. She wasn't sure why I'd invited her to this so-called concert that I was playing in.

Wayne was also a student of Igor Lazko, and went just before me. Luckily for me, he was also a very decent pianist. So, when he went on, Julie became more relaxed, thinking that I might not be such a joke after all. She thought that they'd saved the best for last. I played Chopin's *Nocturne Op.9 No.3*, Prokofiev's *Piano Sonata No. 2*, and the final prelude and fugue by Shostakovich. Julie was so impressed. I think this was the moment she fell in love with me. Just like that, we decided that we were going to get married. Of course, this is my perspective on things.

After this concert, she started to become even more interested in my life. I told her everything that had happened in my life up to then. This was a week before I was to head back to Singapore for the holidays as I'd planned. I could afford to go home and I was on better terms with my mom, so I was looking forward to going home. I had five days after the concert to go home and things were blossoming between Julie and I, so I knew it wasn't going to be as easy to go as it would have been had I not met her. In the days that followed, we really fell deeply for each other.

One of those days included me taking her on a date to a seafood restaurant. It was an expensive restaurant and I was happy to take her given that I was making some money now. However, I still had the same attitudes and did things the same way. I never saved. I would spend every penny I made and I didn't realise that I had spent almost all my money until my card declined when I tried to pay the restaurant bill. Julie paid the bill for us.

The day before going to this restaurant, I had brought her to Disney Land and spent most of the money I had in my account, so I had insufficient funds. While at Disney Land, I put my arms around her, showing her that I was very interested in us being together. By then, I had already been telling my friends that she was going to be my girlfriend. I guess she fell for it as I managed to hold her hand soon after while I was bringing her to work. Every day, I would bring her to work, then from work to lunch, and from lunch back to work. I didn't have a car, so we would take the metro together wherever we went.

I went back to Singapore and told my parents about my girlfriend. Of course, I couldn't tell them that I had only met her three weeks earlier and was planning to marry her. As a Christian, there was no playing when it comes to saying that I was dating. It meant that I wanted her to be my wife someday.

While in Singapore, I kept in touch with Julie through Skype. She decided to come to Singapore to visit me. She came for one week and we went to Kuala Lumpur together, which was my first holiday in the longest of times. Then we went back to Paris together, she to her internship and me to school. Back in Paris, Julie and I started working on building our relationship and getting to know each other even more. She would follow me to my concerts and I kept walking her to and from work. We spent a year together in Paris. Of course, like most couples, as we got to know each other, we had disputes and fun times. For example, she's very family oriented having grown up in a family that is close and open with each other while I am not, also because of my upbringing. I'm very independent. I have looked after myself and lived overseas more than half my life. Her family helps each other and looks after each other. On the other hand, my only support system in my family was my mom and that wasn't even stable.

By 2012, I was performing in a lot of piano competitions and I wasn't doing very well in school. It's strange because every time I fall in love, I don't do well in other aspects of my life, which I find very interesting. I still managed to take home some prizes but I wasn't winning like I used to. Of about twenty competitions, I only won three first prizes. In all honesty, I do find these competitions often unfair. There were times when I would play very average and get to the semifinals. While there were times when I'd play extremely well and believed that I'd get to the next round, but don't. One such time was when I went to a piano competition in Slovenia. In my opinion, that was one of the best concerts I have ever played. I felt really good about the prospects of winning or at least being placed in the top three. However, I was placed sixth. François Weigel, who was one of the jury members, was so upset that he protested and resigned from the competition; he didn't think that the judging was fair. He'd given me full marks, as he also thought that I should have won the competition. This gave my confidence a well-needed boost. All my tutelage and hard work was paying off in one way or another.

I flunk so many exams that year. My French was not good by any means. I had learned most of it with the kids I was staying with, so it was very informal and lack the proper structure that it needed. I flunk my analysis exam, the history of music exam, and my harmony test. I kept doing well in things that were performance related. The only thing I knew how to do was play the piano. I did well in chamber music exam, proving that I had really learned to listen, accompany, and accommodate other musicians as Nina had taught me.

I also did very well in my sight reading exam. Christine was my sight reading teacher. She was from Rouen and was very strong headed. She'd come to class and shout at everyone in their face. She managed a class of seven to eight of us on different instruments—two on the violin, one on the flute, one on the cello, two on the piano, one on the saxophone, and so on. I don't know how she did it, but if one of us made a mistake, she would not miss it. She would know exactly who it was although we were all playing at the same time.

To me, Christine looked like someone who was drinking music rather than listening to it. I was so baffled by her skills that I asked her one day how she was able to spot who had made a mistake so easily while we were all playing at the same time. She explained to me that each time she came to class—she'd take a ninety-minute train ride from Rouen to Paris—and she would read her scores on the train, so she knew who was playing what and when. I was still baffled even after her explanation.

I remember always coming out of her lessons with tears in my eyes and my heart beating two times faster. I was so scared of her but she never criticized how I played the piano. She told me once, "I am not here to teach you how to play the piano, I am here to teach you how to read music," and she did exactly that. She transformed my way of looking at music. I used to read music note by note like a machine. However, she revolutionised the way I think about music.

She told me that one doesn't need an instrument to play music because the music is within us. You can hear the music before you play the music. Like a movie director, you don't have the crew, the characters, the materials, the equipment to create your scene that you need, but you already know what you want to see, how you want the movie to be. You know when you want the girl to cry; when you want the couple to kiss; you know what you want to happen when. So, by the time you get everything together to make the movie, you are not here to try, you are here to perform.

She told me to practise sitting in a room reading only my score and playing the music in my mind. Then when I was done with that, to go back to playing the piano and see how it transformed how I played. I decided to try.

Christine never said anything nice about me either. She would just go crazy at everyone throughout her entire lesson. At the end of the year, I got thirteen point five over the score of twenty. Ten was the passing mark. Levels were very high but the highest anyone got for sightreading was fourteen. I went to see her after my exam. I was very prepared. I had done what she suggested—practising in my head for five minutes before playing the piece—and it worked. When I saw her after the exam, she said, "I always knew you would do it." I was shocked as I thought, *There is no way you always knew when you always screamed at me so much in your class.* Of course, I didn't say that out loud.

My first time at Disney Land Paris with Julie

With Igor Lasko

A public masterclass with Éric Heidsieck

Score by Éric Heidsieck

With François Weigel

Congyu Wang, un jeune pianiste lumineux

JEU. Musicien complet, Congyu Wang a déjà de très nombreux festivals, concerts et récitals de part le monde, à son actif.

Il n'a que vingt ans, et... dix-sept ans d'étude du piano derrière lui. Il a ouvert samedi de façon magistrale les 13e Rencontres musicales de La Verrerie.

Congyu Wang a fait montre de façon lumineuse de son immense talent de pianiste, faisant vivre des moments extraordinaires à l'auditoire. Sa maîtrise de l'instrument est impressionnante. Il est vrai que le jeune pianiste singapourien a été à bonne école ces dernières années se perfectionnant dès 2008, grâce à une bourse d'étude pour la prestigieuse école normale de musique de Paris Alfred Cortot,

auprès de deux pianistes de renom, Jean Marc Luisada et Odile Catelin-Delangle.

À la suite, il intégrera la Schola Cantorum pour approfondir encore ses connaissances auprès de l'unique élève de Francis Poulenc, Gabriel Tachino. Samedi, son interprétation splendide et délicate de l'improvisation 5 de Francis Poulenc a ébloui.

Il avait ouvert le concert sur le Prélude 5 et l'Étude n° 5, *Pour les octaves* de Claude Debussy interprétant ces œuvres avec une virtuosité impressionnante.

La nocturne OP.33 n° 3 de Fauré achevait de convaincre par un jeu léger et tout en finesse. En deuxième partie, le pianiste mit à l'honneur quatre compositions de Chopin dont il connaît les intégrales à la perfection, comme celles de Poulenc. Un pianiste lumineux d'aisance. ■

Prochain concert. Samedi 21 avril, à 18 h 30, avec le pianiste Ferenc Vizi et la violoncelliste Hermine Horiot. Au programme, Schubert et Chopin. Tél. 02.48.81.51.80.

The review of my first public ticketed concert at the Château de la Verrerie – a gift François

Photo taken at the concert

With Aquiles Delle Vigne

One of my first concerts in France playing at the Chalon-
sur-Saône

My first birthday dinner with Julie

CHAPTER 13

I AM IN SWITZERLAND WHERE I am playing at a concert tonight. With running around preparing for the concert all of yesterday, I completely forgot about sorting out my suit. There are only six hours left before I take my seat at the piano, and I remember that I still have to get it ironed. The original plan was to get the hotel's laundry service to do it for me but I haven't, and now there is no way they will be able to get it back to me in time.

I sit in my hotel room on the bed extremely annoyed with myself. I have no idea what I am going to do. I still have too much to do to worry about my suit but there is no way I am wearing it like this. Okay, I have to get everything else ready for the night, so I am going out for a few hours. *Argh!* I scold myself internally. *This should have been sorted yesterday. How did I miss this?*

I spend time ticking things off my to-do list. All done, I make my way back to the hotel room. Back in my suite to shower and get dressed, the suit is still there waiting on me. It still needs to be ironed. With no other option, I get the ironing board and iron from the wardrobe and decide to iron it. I have no other choice; do I?

All of a sudden, I find myself in a fit of laughter. I am laughing at myself, nothing else. Here I am, ironing my own concert attire. I can't help it. I reach for my phone, take a photo of myself, and send it to Jesse. A photo of me ironing my own suit with the caption, "Today you win."

Two Years in Uniform and a Musical Journey

I t was time to go home for the National Service and Julie couldn't come to Singapore because of her internship in Paris. She had a choice to stay in Paris or go to Hong Kong but she stayed in Paris for six more months, so we were going to have to be entirely apart.

In the National Service, it was highly recommended to see a psychiatrist before enlisting, and so I did. In the end, I wasn't enlisted into the army; I was enlisted into the civil defence which is like the paramedics and fire service combined. My job was pretty much in an office. I think because of what I had been through, they didn't think I should be holding any weapons or anything like that. It might all be a coincidence but I was honest about everything I had survived in Paris and I think it might have played a role in my placement.

On the day of my enlistment, they shaved all my hair off to zero. This was the first time that I felt like I was an animal instead of a human being. Yes, even with everything I had been through. The sergeant said to me, "From this day until your service is completed, you are not a citizen of Singapore. You have to earn your right to be a citizen." I thought this was taking things too far. I had already been through so much and here I was being told that I was no longer a citizen of the country that I was born and raised in. There were younger kids than me, imagine how they felt hearing this. Young men, teens, were crying. This was also the first time in my life I'd felt so mature. I'd already been living away from home for almost four years, so I didn't miss home. I didn't need to cry and call my parents but I understood what they were going through.

I wasn't sad. Throughout my time in training, it felt like a holiday camp for me. I had free drinks, free food, free gym equipment, a place to stay, everything. Everything I needed to survive. It was like a holiday getaway where I didn't have to spend my own money. The only sad thing was that during these six weeks in training, I couldn't practice the piano. It felt like the longest period of my life without it, like I was missing out on some kind of drug that I needed.

I was enlisted in what is known as the Singapore Civil Defence Force (SCDF). In this unit, there was this training camp that they called Civil Defence Academy. It's similar to when you go to the army where you have to ask for permission for everything as you are being trained by the sergeants and instructors. You can't go to the washroom as and when you want to. You can't decide to go out with your friends as and when you like. Everything had to go through the instructors, and they could decide whether or not you got to do whatever you were requesting permission for.

I was in the Alpha Company. They had a Sergeant Warrant, who was this huge body-builder-looking guy called John, who everyone was afraid of. He went to the gym daily and could do the most bench press and so on. He didn't have to speak for you to be intimidated by him. Most of my time in the service was spent with Curren John who was my boss for two years. He ran a music band as well. Though, technically, on paper, it doesn't exist. Joining the band entailed gaining many benefits. For every performance I played in the band, I would get a day off. When there was rehearsal, which were very few, I also got time off.

This was where I learned to improvise and really play jazz and so many other genres. I had to learn to accompany singers. We had no scores and no time to prepare ahead of playing. Each of us in the band was busy with our own jobs, so we didn't get to meet and rehearse as we'd have liked. We pretty much had to just get on with it, which I didn't mind as it gave me the chance to play regardless.

The band was there to serve just as we each were in our individual job roles while serving. Let's say that the ministers of finance from the Philippines and Singapore were meeting in Singapore. They do not want to pay a professional band, so they would come to the National Service to get us to play. We could play anything. In this case, we would learn some Philippines songs that would have been sent to us via weblinks and we would have to play. This was how I learned how to play music by Bruno Mars, Ella Fitzgerald, Beyonce, the Bee Gees, and the Platters.

We didn't play classical music. Although jazz or pop was not my style of music, it opened up my mind to the different types of music and ways to play. At times, I had to transpose on the spot to accommodate certain singers and that helped me to become a better pianist in so many ways. Today, I am able to show up for a performance with an artist and transpose as necessary. I can play anything, prepared or unprepared, which leaves many doors open for me. I get to play on different platforms, accompanying singers who I sometimes don't get to prepare ahead of time with.

While in this band, I worked with so many people from so many different places all over the world. I knew I would not go this route once I got out of the National Service—play jazz or stay in a band—but it helped me pass the time. Two years would have been impossible otherwise. I mean, two years is a very long time. You can have two kids in two years. I couldn't imagine having no music whatsoever in all that time, so playing jazz in a band was very much welcomed.

In the service, there was a sergeant called Ryan, Sergeant Ryan. When I told him about what I had been through in Paris; he couldn't believe it. He told the entire platoon my story, so my bandmates knew about my life before the service to an extent. I met very good friends in the National Service who are still my friends even now. We live far apart but I still consider them my very good friends. I met Jesse who is still my friend to this day. He was one of my instructors and was also part of the band. He's also a fantastic jazz pianist.

So, there was uniform check done every night and Jesse was responsible for this. We had to iron them to shine and look completely pristine. I thought this was crazy. Who cared whether or not our uniforms were pristine? Well, Alpha had this reputation for being the best recruits, marching the best (traditionally winning the marching competition each intake), the best uniform, everything. Curren John had the highest expectations, so we all had to perform. Knowing Jesse outside of the service now, I know that he is a very funny guy, but of course, in the service as an instructor, he had to be strict and he really was. Jesse would be in his office and we would all take our ironed uniform to him to be checked. If it wasn't ironed properly, you would expect to not go to bed until two a.m. or so because you would have to redo it, which took about two hours.

Jesse knew that I was a classical pianist. When they held the audition to look for musicians, they saw my information that I had graduated from music school in Paris and had a degree in music. Now, the funny thing was that when Jesse was inspecting my uniform one night, he asked, "Do you know that your uniform looks like shit?" At this point, I was a recruit, so I couldn't give my very honest answer which was 'no.' Instead, I told him that I would go re-iron it. Then he asked me, "So, next time, when you are a concert pianist, who is going to iron your uniform for you?" I couldn't stop the words from falling out, "I will take it to the laundrette," I said plainly. I laugh about that now because I really don't iron my own concert clothes, but that night in Switzerland, I had no other choice but to iron it myself.

After the National Service, Jesse went back to university to pursue a degree in sociology. In 2015, he came to one of my concerts, and a couple of months later, he quit university. He went back into music. I remember him saying that life is too short to have regrets and now he's doing very well, composing and performing quite a lot. He's told me a few times that I was the one who inspired him to pursue this dream after I told him after one of my concerts he attended that he could be a great musician, but I think it was just his destiny.

There is so much that music can do that I can't. My music can be so overwhelming and even overwhelms me sometimes. It changes people's lives in ways that I myself can't. I even remember once someone came up to me and said, "You look really young, like you can't be more than twenty-one, but I was just healed by your music. When I sat down at the beginning of your concert, I was feeling the pain in my knee that I have been feeling for many years and now I don't. I can walk out with ease." I am happy that my music can have that effect. Music can heal as well as guide people. Sometimes I think it has a spiritual effect and can be translated in so many ways; it doesn't have to be physical healing. It can be emotional or spiritual healing as well. It can help a heart broken from a relationship or the loss of a pet or friend. I don't think it's the pianist but rather the music.

I am really happy to have met someone like Jesse and he will always be one of my most treasured friends. I am even more happy that he's composing and playing now as his talent is too great to be locked away.

I also met Daim in the National Service and he is still a treasured friend. He taught me how to use an electric keyboard. I didn't know you could do so many things with it. I learned that you could transpose, make different effects of the base, guitar, orchestra background, and so much more. Daim has a mind of a computer. He is like a hard drive. You could mention any song and he would know it and not just the words of the song, but also down to every detail of the music. He could tell you what the base is doing, how every empty space was filled in any music. If you want to make a music band sound good, you go to Daim. He'd enlisted a bit before me, so we spent about a year and seven months together.

Irsyad was a saxophonist who I met in the National Service too; he was in our band as a guitarist because the main guitarist got injured and had to be replaced. We became close friends because we lived in the same neighbourhood and would travel home together on most days. Neville was also part of the band. He was a violin major and now holds a masters in violin but he was in our band because he could also play the piano. He came in when I was going as he would be my replacement when I left. He was a very versatile musician and could even sing in English and Mandarin. He was a very talented guy.

In the two years, I think I played about seventy-five to eighty concerts and got a total of about ninety days off, which I used some of to go perform in concerts or just practice and visit Julie. She moved to Hong Kong to further her studies and she would come visit me in Singapore. When she graduated and moved back to Réunion, I visited her once each year. As long as I got my days off, I was happy.

I was also able to participate in a piano competition in Indonesia, having learned the *Piano Concerto No. 2* by Chopin from my office in camp. This competition took place in Jakarta in 2014 and I won the third prize, playing with an orchestra in the final round. This was one of the strangest experiences in my life—learning the program on an electric piano and memorising the competition program in three weeks. In the first round, I played a modern piece composed by Ananda Sukarlan, Chopin's *Étude Op.25 No.10*, Beethoven's *Piano Sonata Op.110 in Ab Major*, and Liszt's *Rigoletto Paraphrase*.

To this day, I can remember playing in the final round on an overly exposed Fazioli piano; the tone was way too bright. The orchestra couldn't fit onto the stage, so they placed the musicians under the stage on the right hand side of the pianist. The conductor was on the other side of the stage, almost like an opera! I had never played in such a setup before. I will always remember the stress from this experience. Before going on stage, the conductor whispered to me softly, "Don't be nervous; this is my very first time conducting an orchestra." I died a little bit on the inside! I thought, *Oh my god! It's going to be a mess. There can't be a first for everything. I have to be looking in the opposite direction of where I normally do, and now this. It's just going to be a mess.* Of course, I managed to keep the freaking out on the inside and played the best I could, taking the third prize. I was happy I won a free holiday—'a get out of jail free card' I called it. It gave me the chance to go away and get my mind off the National Service and spend time with the piano instead.

Music was my constant company during my time in the National Service. If I wasn't playing it with the band or practicing, it was on my mind. I wanted a music career and I knew I needed to find a way to make it happen. I decided to send out emails to different managers with a proposal for them to manage me as a pianist. Some didn't respond, others outright rejected my proposal, then I got a response from Carles Lama, who became my concert manager and mentor. He later requested that I create an album, something I hadn't done before but wanted to do.

With the days off I had accumulated in the two years of service, I spent the remaining days recording my debut album. I had to recall all the things I'd learnt in Paris and remind myself of who I really was. National Service had changed me. I was definitely much less effective in my practice and I had been cut off from the real world for almost two years but, deep down, I was Congyu and I was going to become a pianist. That was my dream.

I recorded my first album, *Charme,* with the KNS classical label created by Carles. I had very little time to prepare for this recording, to be honest, I was sight reading some of these music in the studio. The main reason for the lack of practice was due to the fact that I was simultaneously preparing for my wedding ceremony.

The system took a while to enlist me in the National Service. I believe it took an entire year. During this year, I was teaching piano to random students in Singapore. I taught mostly beginners. I had a mixture of students in terms of ages and level of playing and would go to their homes to teach them. I had this experience where I felt like I was underpaid. A lot of people used my name to make huge profits. They would charge learners far more than they would pay me. Then, when I finally started serving, the allowance in the National Service was extremely low. If I remember well, I was making about four hundred

Singaporean dollars per month. This was how I learned to be spendthrift, that I couldn't spend every penny I made. I had to save for my wedding and I did it.

After completing my term in the National Service in May, I got married in June and July. I got married once in Singapore and again in the Réunion. We decided to move to the Réunion because of my wife's family business. They own an Asian supermarket called Asia Store. They sell pretty much all you would find in an Asian supermarket. When I came here, there wasn't a piano for me to work on. I ended up on the island without an instrument, and for a while, I thought that I would never play the piano again.

I started working in Julie's family business. I remember delivering rice to restaurants and driving the truck to carry different products for delivery. I was a delivery man, and at another point, I was taking business trips to Asia to order different products. It offered financial stability but I felt empty. I felt like this wasn't what I was born to do. I wasn't meant to do this kind of physical job or work in an office. I wondered what would happen to all the piano skills that I had spent years acquiring. I believe I did this for a year. Then one day, I was floating in the swimming pool at home, on my back, looking up at the sky. I thought of what I would have done if I wasn't married—the places I would have gone. I decided later that day to write them down on a piece of paper, and today, I have been to most of them, which are marked with colour coded flags on my Google Maps app.

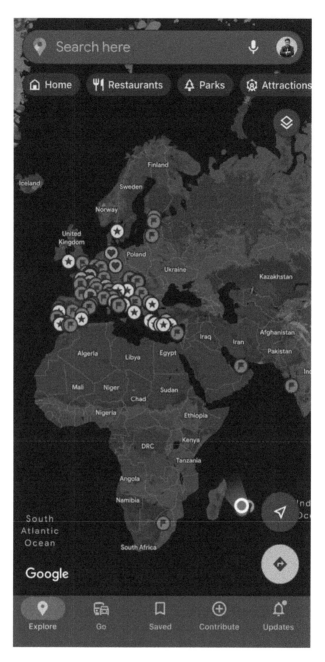

My Google Maps app with tags

214

Performing in a shopping centre at the West Coast in Singapore, while waiting to be enlisted in the National Service

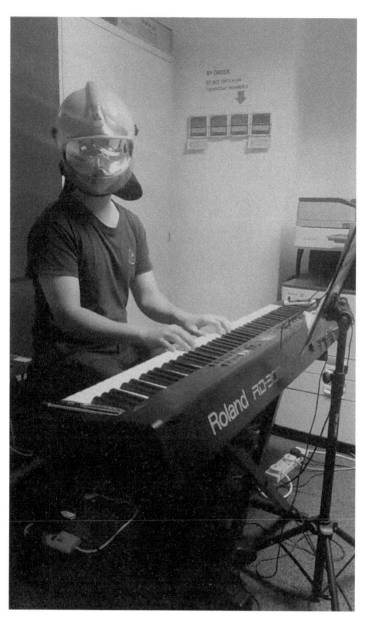

Practising the piano while on duty

With Carles and Sofia. My manager and mentor when I was released from the National Service

My first album

It was also while waiting to be enlisted in the National Service that I was nominated as a Young Steinway Artist, which didn't come by easily. Interestingly, the first time I touched a Steinway, I was fourteen years old. The piano was in a showroom at the Millennial Walk shopping centre. Back then, it was a very old and run down mall and Steinway was being run by a different company. A Steinway piano wouldn't be out on the shop floor. It would be in its box packed away. There was an old lady in the shop. I remember being with a couple of my friends heading back from the music library. The shopping centre was just next to the library. We asked the lady if we could sample the piano. I told her that I wanted to play on the Steinway because I hadn't played on one before. She looked at me with such arrogance as she said, "You should try playing on a Yamaha or something else, you will never be able to afford a Steinway."

I wasn't going to give in. I wanted to play on it too bad. I told her, "I'll come back with my mother and you will allow me to play," and I left the shop with my friends. I did indeed go back with my mother. When she opened up the box and allowed me to play on the Steinway, I was attached to it immediately. Everything about it was exquisite. It wasn't like any other piano that I had ever played on. I wanted to keep playing. In that very moment, it became a life goal; I needed one for myself and promised myself that I would own a Steinway piano one day.

The lady was extremely nasty to me. She told me how horribly I played and ridiculed me, saying that I played like I was in a market place. "Terrible playing. Terrible playing," she said multiple times with disgust evident on her face. I was so disappointed with this sales person that even if I had the money to buy the piano at the time, I wouldn't have bought it from her. Nominated as a Young Steinway Artist at the age of twenty-one, I recalled this incident well. Here I was being nominated to represent the same brand that she thought I would never be able to afford. I wonder what she would have thought if she'd known that I was that same young boy.

When I graduated from École Normale and went back to Singapore, I wanted to buy myself a piano because I had never owned one. Of course, me being me, I wanted the best of the best. I wanted a Steinway but I couldn't afford it. I'd also wanted to become a Steinway Artist and knew that I also had to own a Steinway & Sons piano to even be considered. By this time, Steinway had its own showroom in Singapore. I met the general manager, Celine, who introduced me to Andrew. He is also Singaporean and worked as a sales representative then. Now he heads the Steinway & Sons operations in Thailand.

There are many requirements to becoming a Steinway Artists, many of which I didn't meet yet. I had just graduated from music school and didn't have an extensive portfolio. I was very young, and most other Steinway Artists were already well-established and in their forties and over.

So, although I wanted to become a Steinway Artist, I also didn't meet the main requirement; I didn't own a Steinway & Sons piano. I was only 20, and as you know by now, I didn't have that kind of money. The piano would have cost at least one hundred thousand dollars. Andrew, who had heard about my leaving Singapore as a teenager to pursue my music dreams in Paris was impressed by my drive and offered his support to help me become a Young Steinway Artist. Andrew thought I was convicted in my wanting to become a pianist and representing Steinway. He told me that there was an alternative to meeting the requirement of having a Steinway piano. He sold me a more affordable Boston piano to be able to qualify in that regard. Buying the Boston piano, which is a subsidiary for the Steinway, gave me the platform to be nominated to become a Young Steinway Artist. Celine nominated me. It was my first step into the world of Steinway—a world I always knew I wanted to be part of.

I was grateful for the help that Andrew and his team provided me in becoming a Young Steinway Artist. As you already know by now, I like impressing, and with such an honour, I was going to treat Andrew and the others to something special. We went to Fosters Steakhouse in Holland Village. I appreciated their help. It was more than selling me a piano and helping with the processing of becoming a Young Steinway Artist. I had a huge dream of not just becoming a pianist but also being aligned with a brand that I had admired from childhood, and they were helping me with that. Becoming a Young Steinway Artist, which wasn't easy for me, opened many doors for me in my career and continue to help me live out my dream—that's not something I can pay them back for and surely not with an expensive dinner.

The lady I met when I was a child was the worst and only terrible attendant I have met selling a Steinway. Everywhere I have gone where they sell Steinway, they have all been kind, often allowing me to play in their shops. I've made very good friends with the Steinway network. It is a good platform to be on to meet the right people. Steinway would invite their VIP guests to my concerts and that's how I made a lot of contacts who would also become my sponsors for my festivals. I am pleased that I did not allow that one bad experience at the age of fourteen to deter me from the brand that I love. I didn't allow it to interfere with my connection with the instrument.

Official Young Steinway Artist nominee photo

With Ádám György as he conferred me the Young Steinway
Artist title

Arduous trek scaling musical heights

By SARA YAP

EVERY teenager goes through a rebellious phase, but local pianist Wang Congyu took this to a whole new level when he ran away from home and flew to Paris to enrol in a prestigious music school. All without speaking a word of French or having much money on him after using up his savings for the plane ticket.

Wang, then 16, had snagged a scholarship to the École Normale de Musique de Paris, but his parents objected to him accepting it because they felt he was too young to go alone to France.

After mulling over the issue for a few days, Wang decided that the opportunity was too precious to pass up, and left without even sitting his O Level exams.

"I had mixed feelings at first," he recalls. "A part of me felt really bad. My friends were busy studying for their exams and there I was, trying to be a pianist and getting my parents worried. But on the other hand, I don't regret what I did, because I came from a sheltered background, and leaving home forced me to grow up."

The gamble paid off. On Tuesday, Wang, 21, was named the second Singaporean recipient of the Young Steinway Artist title. Hungarian pianist Adam Gyorgy, who is also Wang's mentor, formally awarded him the title at the Steinway Gallery in Palais Renaissance.

The first local pianist to receive the award was Abigail Sin in 2009. It provides opportunities for young talented pianists and offers them access to Steinway & Sons' resources.

Wang recalls how challenging his early days in Paris were: he led an almost nomadic lifestyle during his first year there, as he had nowhere to live and little money. The scholarship covered only his school fees; he was expected to take care of his own living expenses.

"I couldn't rent an apartment as I was underaged. I had to beg people to let me stay with them," says Wang. "Nothing was easy. A few times, I even thought of going back to Singapore."

He shuttled between friends' homes before meeting a family at church. They let him live with them for the remainder of his time in Paris.

And there was another problem: finding a piano to practise on.

"Once, I was staying at a friend's home for a while and he had a piano. His French neighbours actually signed a petition to kick us out of the apartment because we were practising all day, and they didn't like it. After that incident, I didn't get to practise on a piano for a very long time," he says.

"At one point, I got so desperate that I carved piano keys on a table so I could 'practise' on them," he says.

Having won piano competitions in Bordeaux and Berlin, graduating last year with a Diplome Superieur from the Schola Cantorum de Paris – another private school he attended – and receiving the Steinway title, Wang has come a long way.

"I never thought I would make it this far. Some people call it destiny and some call it fate, but I call it God's plan," he says.

He adds that his parents were unhappy in the beginning but they grew supportive when they saw he was serious about pursuing his love of music.

Steinway Gallery Singapore's general manager Celine Goh, who had nominated Wang for the award, says his talent and determination were what convinced her that he was right for the Young Steinway Artist title.

"I was impressed by his track record and future plans. He has also won prestigious competitions, and he has both the foundation and a good personality. I feel that he is someone who can represent the Steinway brand well," she says.

> 'At one point, I got so desperate that I carved piano keys on a table so I could 'practise' on them.'
>
> – Winner Wang Congyu on his trials in Paris pursuing music where he had no piano at one point to practise on. (Below) Hungarian pianist Adam Gyorgy with Wang and Steinway Gallery Singapore's general manager Celine Goh

PHOTO: STEINWAY GALLERY SINGAPORE

Article about receiving the Young Steinway Artist title

With Lang Lang

My last day in the National Service

CHAPTER 14

"**WHAT DO YOU MEAN YOU'RE** playing on top of a mountain? Is there a concert hall up there?" Julie asks, confusion etched on her face.

"I don't have all the details yet, but so far, it seems that I will be playing outside on the actual mountain."

"Huh? And who's going to be listening to you? How will you even get up there? You don't hike…"

I laugh because she's right—I don't hike—but more so because of the expression on her face. I am also trying to make sense of it. I've said yes to the concert but I haven't given it as much thought as Julie is doing right now. The idea of playing on a mountain is in and of itself quite interesting. I am intrigued.

A few weeks later, Julie and I arrive at the airport and are chauffeured to the hotel. It's a beautiful hotel suite and I wish we were staying a few days. I am having back to back events. Tomorrow when I get back from this concert, I will be off to judge a piano competition and the next few days will be extremely busy, but for now, we are going to embrace this experience.

After a good night's rest, we awake and get ready for the day. We spend most of the day together enjoying each other's company before we have to get ready for the concert. Another chauffer picks us up at the hotel and we are being driven again to another destination. Soon, we arrive at this place in Rivière des Galets where we meet our host. It's a huge playing field where a helicopter is waiting. We aren't quite sure yet why it is there or why we are out here on this huge field.

We aren't hiking up the mountain! We are being taken by the helicopter that's waiting, our host tells us. Julie and I whisper among ourselves. We aren't even sure it is safe to fly from here but we agree that we'll take this leap of faith. I mean, we only live once and all that.

I am unsure whether I would have hiked like the four hundred people who are hiking up the mountain for this concert as we speak. In all honesty, I probably would for a pianist I really wanted to see.

Julie and I boarded the helicopter and were soon in flight. Seeing the valleys from this point of view is spectacular. The pilot soon let us know that we are coming up to the mountain on our left. It is on Julie's side and we both turn to see it. I wasn't told how the piano would get there before now, so seeing the other helicopter already landed on the mountain top and the piano being offloaded holds my attention, and Julie's. We are both amazed by the organisers who are pulling together this event. They had an idea and I am watching it unfold before my eyes. Below us, we are told, the colours we see rounding the mountain are the attendees trekking up to see me play.

I'm mesmerised. I can't wait to land. The idea of being so engrossed in nature with music is exciting on so many levels. I never imagined in my wildest dreams that I would be on such an adventure.

We finally alight the helicopter that landed a few moments ago two thousand feet above ground level and are ushered to where the piano is being set up. Before I know it, people have taken seats on the mountain at this free concert picnic style. It's three a.m. in the morning and I am playing the four Chopin Ballades under candle light next to the piano.

A few days after the concert on the mountain, I finish playing in a concert hall and go to meet people from the crowd. These two old ladies come up to me and one asks, "Where do you live? Where are you from?"

"I am originally from Singapore but I live in the Réunion," I say.

"Wow!" her companion enthuses. "Where did you study?"

At the exact same time, the other asks, "At what age did you start playing the piano?"

The three of us chuckle. "I studied in Paris at Ecole Normale but before that, I learned to play in Singapore."

"Aww!" one of the women let out and covers her mouth.

"What is it?" her companion asks exactly what I was thinking.

"It's him!"

"Who?" the other returns.

She turns to me saying, "Do you know, we were just at your concert on the mountain. We climbed it to see you because we just wanted to know who you are. We just wanted to see you…"

"Oh wow, it really is you? Yes, we were there at your concert. We really wanted to see you and thought we would only get to see you on the mountain, so we hiked all the way. Here you are again! What a treat! I can't believe it." She laughs with her companion.

I can't get a word in as the two of them are so excited, filling in parts of this story they are sharing with me. Apparently, tonight they took some time to recognise me because I look different from the way I did on the mountain. My tuxedo was throwing them off earlier. One of them was confused the entire time I was playing, sure that she'd heard me play before but she wasn't sure where.

We talk some more as they ask me so many different questions about my life and my playing. Standing there with them, answering all their questions, I am overcome with an inner peace because I know exactly what this means…

It's in the Music

I grew up as a young child with very stereotypical thinking. I thought that the piano was for girls and so was the harp. I didn't see the use of playing either of them. Although I started playing from around age three, I actually hated the piano. I literally hated it. As you've read in earlier chapters, it wasn't until the age of thirteen that I discovered or rather fell in love with the piano. Even though I hated it, I played it good enough. I could play by ear, which I thought was pretty good. I could read music and didn't have to practice for many hours to learn something.

I don't know if having a gift is something that you are born with or it is something that you develop. Maybe it is something that you discover or rediscover at a later age like I did. Regardless, I think a gift is something that you begin to understand when you have the correct instrument and the right amount of encouragement to do what you want to do in life.

Even talent isn't one thing. It's not something that you are good at doing. Talent is a package. You need to have interest in doing something for you to even call it a talent. You can be a very good cook but what if you just don't like to eat? Talent is not one skillset. It is a package. To be good at the piano, you can't just be good at it. You have to practice; you have to be thirsty; you have to always want to improve yourself. It's also very much about personality: a boring person can never be a talented person. Talent is everything to do with you as the person. You have to have the will to want to do what you want to be good at. There is no talent without will.

God gave me my gift as a way to connect with people, something that I have been able to do in ways that I never imagined. However, that gift on its own wasn't going to do what I am able to do with my music today. He sent me on a journey to help me become the full package. Looking back, God made me go through everything I have been through because he wanted my music to be more colourful. All the suffering that I had to go through makes my music more real and more sincere. I now understand people from different backgrounds. Music can only be shared from within and it brings people from different walks of life together. I understand people of all walks of life because I was so many of them or interacted with so many of them at different times in my life. I've been homeless begging for food on the street and I've dined with some of the greatest people of our time. I've lived on both extremes and in between.

God brought people into my life to teach me things that would make me the person I am today. Jean-Marc taught me how to share. In music, you share with your hearing, in a restaurant, you share with your sense of taste, and in the movies, you share with your eyes. These three art forms all have one thing in common; they all touch your heart. Sometimes you hear something in the movies and you are so touched by it. It's personal. You smell something and you think about your grandmother. You go to a restaurant and eat very good pasta and you think of all the times when you had to eat the worst possible pasta ever! It transports you to a time and place.

It is the same with music. Your hearing is more difficult to stimulate, but with music, as the musician, you have to be more connected with your audience on a deeper level. If you don't have the message you want to communicate with the audience listening to you, then they might as well listen to a CD rather than go to a concert. The only thing that connects you to the audience is the connection of sharing what you feel and want them to feel. I learned from Jean-Marc to not think about what music can bring to your life but to think rather what your life can bring to music. He didn't teach me this with words but more so with the expulsion from his class which was the biggest punishment I have had as a human being—not being able to get a second chance. It took me years to heal. I would only find comfort in the church and later in meeting my wife. Today, I am able to bring all of myself to music in the way that I believe is best for me.

A full house concert in 2019

CHAPTER 15

A FEW DAYS AGO, I signed a contract with Seabourn Cruise Line to play on a number of their cruise ships through to 2025. This is one of the biggest achievements thus far in my career. One that I am grateful for and look forward to enjoying.

Now I'm aboard one of their ships to play. It's mid-afternoon and we are doing the setup. I am with the technicians who are in the sound box checking the lights and everything. They usually have different colour lights on the set; it's normal. Normally, they ask about the lighting that one wants; dimmer lighting, bright lights, or colour lighting. They are playing with the colours during my rehearsal to give me the chance to choose my preference. I ask them to choose the bright light—the brightest one. It is a bright white light and seems perfect. I also ask them to not change the lighting while I am playing, as is sometimes done, because it affects my playing significantly. I know that now.

As I am there practising, the light keeps changing and so did my playing. There are so many colours that they didn't even show me earlier. I mean, I just asked them to not change the lighting and explained why, yet the lights keep changing. I turn and almost yell at the technician, "Can you stop changing the lighting, please?"

He replies, with the most confused look on his face, "I wasn't changing the lighting. What are you talking about?"

I don't have a response for him. I just stop in my tracks and soon have to take in what is happening. I need to process. The lights were changing as I was playing. I have no reason to mistrust him, though. I look down at the piano keys and they are black and white again. The light is exactly what I asked for and the technician is standing exactly where he just replied to me. He didn't change them back.

The colour of the keys were changing as I played. It wasn't the lighting. They were changing with the music.

I am aboard a huge ship with a lot of luxury. I started the day with a few mimosas, so I am feeling quite emotional. I sit there and take that information in. I am feeling and that's what matters. I am having a good time aboard this ship with my wife. That's all it is. Today the music is beautiful. Today it's positive and I am seeing a beautiful variety of colours and shapes.

Sitting on the piano bench, I inhale a deep breath and for the first time in all these years, I purposefully take myself back to being a seventeen-year-old teen on the streets of Paris feeling so lost in my homelessness. I go back because for the very first time, I have true understanding. It is only now that I understood why the music had stopped inside me then. I had stopped seeing the colours inside my head because my dream of becoming a musician was threatened in so many ways; not just by being homeless but also from losing my piano teacher. The music had stopped in my head because its entire future was threatened. Without music, I am indeed nothing. I am one with the music and I feel every bit of it.

I Get it Now

I see colours when I hear music, actually, when I hear any noise. Sounds come to me in colours and shapes. That's how my mind interprets what I am hearing. It took me a long time to understand this fact. Growing up, I had a wild imagination. I used to think that I couldn't differentiate colours in real life. However, when I closed my eyes, I would see those colours clearly. I could close my eyes to try to understand the sounds I was hearing and would see colours. This included blue and green, where I would be able to tell the difference. Same with purple and brown. In reality though, when I looked around me, the colours were always changing from what they really were. I also realised when I was really young that when music affects my emotional state, especially if it is extremely intense, when I closed my eyes really tightly and blinked very hard, I would see shapes. Like fruits such as strawberries, watermelons, all kinds of different shapes, and every one of them would come with a colour.

I didn't realise it at the time. In fact, it took me many years to stop and look at what was happening. If the music was deeply saddening, I would see greys or black and white. When the music was happy, however, like Mozart, I would see pinks, light blues, and yellowish colours. I didn't realise it then but this started from a very young age. Although I wasn't a musical child, I was always in touch with music. My father liked classical music, so we listened to a lot of it in our house. Plus my sister played the piano and violin and would play at home. Still, I wasn't as deeply affected at that young age. Maybe I just didn't notice or understand it.

As I got more and more connected to music on a personal level, through playing, I realised how sensitive I am to music and pretty much everything I hear. Music enhances my senses. I get even more affected when I go through difficult things in my life like the break up I went through back in secondary school or when we were going through things in our family.

With age and experience, I learned to understand this effect better. I know how which music or sound affects me. I can't control all the sounds around me but I can control what happens with the piano to a great extent. That's why I keep going back to the piano. I can choose what I feel. Every time I play, I get to choose my colours. When I feel really sad and don't have anyone to talk to, I don't make my life worse by wallowing in those sad emotions, I go to the piano and I play. I help myself to deal with those emotions by choosing soothing or happy music that improves my mood. I choose what I play, and that allows me to see the colours that make me whole again. Colours that bring back the joy into my life. Sometimes, I also play music that's not so exciting but I know how to play them so I don't dig myself into a bigger hole.

In classical music especially, we have a lot of minor music, which is very sad music. It's tragic. Like love letters in the nineteenth century that was so dramatic and romantic. However, you get the chance to think of it in a different way if you play with a different approach, which is something I have had to learn along the way.

When I was sixteen or seventeen, I was a typical teenager, playing everything really loud, really fast; I wanted my music to sound impressive. However, with age and time, I learned to be more tamed and more in control of my music. I learned to be wiser in terms of my performance. I learned to be in control of myself. In essence, I do not 'cry my heart out' every time I play music. I stay in control and decide what aspects of the music I want to boaster. By doing that, I am able to see the colours more as they are. What I mean by this is that I see the music as it is meant to be seen. For the composers, why did they compose the music to sound that way? Every music I play is like a message from the composer to the listener. That's how I really learned to appreciate music in itself.

Unfortunately, there are many other components that affect how you play and how the music is heard by the listener as well. The actual instrument is one of them.

Now, you must know that I have no bias; it's simply my reality. I fell in love with the Steinway from a very young age and have always favoured pianos by Steinway & Sons. However, as I got older, my preference became more because of Steinway's performance. It is pretty much the crème de la crème of pianos in my book. With other pianos, sometimes the music isn't precise and the performance is not as good. The Steinway on the other hand is always extremely close to perfection, and I do mean extremely close. Comparing it to other pianos, it's like trying to bake a cake in the best oven available and another in a standard oven. The batter will be the exact same but the cake baked in the best possible oven will always produce a better cake in the end. It might even be that you get a crappy end product with the standard oven. It is the same with the Steinway. The music gets interpreted as I want it to be. The colours are as they should be and what I want them to be. I can produce the exact colours that I want to see every single time without fail. What I hear in my mind is what I play. It helps me to anticipate the sound and interpret it through my playing. Thus, whatever it is that I want to play in my mind is what comes off the keys when I play. I know how much weight I have to play on a note for it to sound loud, soft, sexy, mushy, or mysterious. There are so many notes to play on the piano and without the best instrument, you're not able to get so close to the intention of what it is that you want to communicate. For example, if you are playing a very sad piece of music where the colours are very dull, and life is very slow and everyone starts watching you, in that moment, when everyone slows down is where the magic needs to happen. That takes me back to something that my teacher often said to me. Basically, if at the end of the concert, someone comes to see you and say, "Oh, that was an interesting concert," you have played the worse concert ever. However, if they come up to you and say, "How do you play the piano like that?" If they want to know where you lived and learned to play the piano, then you are doing something right. You are communicating the music to your audience. Steinway allows me to do that every single time. After every concert, these are the sentiments that I receive and hence why you are reading this book now.

I am not a Primadona, however. In any regard. Even with all my success up to now, I don't have to fly first class or business class. If I turn up to a concert to play and I don't get to play on a Steinway, I won't 'act up.' I will play my concert because it is important to play. I have learned to deal with it over the years. I have had to play on a digital piano during National Service. I have turned up to play the piano and gotten forty year old pianos to play on where I couldn't even feel the ivory on the keys. It is tough to play with such an instrument and I end up feeling like I am walking on eggshells but you don't always get to choose your instrument. Just like you don't get to choose your audience or any of the other factors involved.

As a pianist, I am relaxed. I just want to play, so the conditions don't actually matter. For example, I will go to play in Italy and from the moment I get off the plane I'm at work. There will be someone waiting for me with a board with my name on it. Usually, they don't speak a word of English and my only two Italian words are ciao and grazie. However, I will go with them because they have my name on a board and I know they are there to get me. They take me to my hotel and when I get there, all I usually have is a piece of paper that tells me when rehearsal is and when my concert is. In essence, I have no interaction with anyone. I have no idea who the organiser is, who will be in the audience; I usually know nothing. It's work and I just show up for work and get the job done. I play my concert and know when my flight is leaving. I get dropped at the airport for my flight out and that's it; ciao, ciao, bye, bye.

That's the business of music. You don't meet anyone. When you're at work, you eat dinner alone unless you make plans for yourself. So what brand the piano is isn't that important. You just need a piano. Sometimes, that's just the life of an artist. You just go with the flow. You're on the road and you make things work. It won't pay to be a Primadona and I can't expect everyone to have a Steinway when I go to play. There was a time when I also couldn't afford one.

The other part of being in this business is that it's not always dependent on you or the instrument. The audience also has their part to play. Sometimes, you have a good day; people love you. They clap loudly and scream for you. They are like gladiators shouting in an opera hall. Other times, you have a very bad day. Even though you play very well, the audience are like people above the age of eighty and they have a hard time clapping for you. You can't hear the applause.

Last year for example, I played in Gothenburg. It was freezing and no one clapped after my playing. The organisers kept asking me to play again, to do an encore piece. I said no, telling them that I didn't think the crowd liked me. Very recently, I played in China and that was a bizarre experience. When you play in China, people are playing on their phones as you play. Some are filming you on live social media or talking to their friends, laughing; it's like playing in a circus with all the noise. I've learned to play by ear and go with the flow. Do what is possible during your performance. One of my organiser and friend told me once, "If you can perform in China, you can perform anywhere," and I took that as a compliment. I have played so many concerts in China to date. Nowadays, if I play in China and even hear a baby crying in the concert hall, I just keep playing. There is no guarantee that I will have a silent hall to play in, so I keep playing. The thing is that I have learned to adapt and I am willing to do anything to live out my musical dream. As long as I am playing, I am happy.

My debut with Seabourn, the ultra-luxurious cruise line

In Pamukkale, Turkey with Seabourn

A concert in Sweden

A concert in Gothenburg

A concert at the Royal Palace of Gödöllő in Budapest

A concert in Foshan China

A concert in San Remo, Italy – playing *Mozart Concerto No.20 k.466*

In Mykonos with Seabourn

Focusing on getting the rehearsal done before a concert in the Réunion

Playing at the concert

A concert in Dubai

Playing for BRED at their corporate event

CHAPTER 16

BOARDING THE PLANE IN ITALY, my heart is in turmoil. Mixed emotions swirl within me like a tempestuous sea. Could this reunion be the right thing to do? Six long years have passed since we last spoke, and the wounds from our fractured relationship still run deep. I thought I had healed completely, but since reconnecting on Facebook, I have been somewhat on edge. I don't want this person to walk back into my life then out again.

I soon find myself lost in thought. Memories of our shared past come rushing at me, and the hurtful words that tore us apart play like a movie reel in my mind. Can this reunion truly heal the wounds that time failed to mend? Will he welcome me with open arms, or we never be even a fraction close as we used to be?

The anticipation grows as my flight nears its destination. Paris, the city that chewed me up and spat me out in so many ways, now holds a different kind of promise for me.

I step off the plane and into the bustling Charles de Gaulle Airport; my heart races. Trepidation washes over me, and I feel a fear of the unknown. Deep down, I'm holding on to what seems to be a mustard seed of hope, a longing to reconnect with the person who once was my mentor and confidant.

I make my way to his new address; he now lives in Passy, which is closer to the Eiffel Tower. The building now looms before me, and I hesitate at the threshold. The weight of our past hangs heavy in the air.

I am an expected guest and allowed to make my way to his apartment. Outside the door, I take a deep breath, ready to accept whichever way this goes. Then, at the very moment I am about to knock on the door, it opens and I am face to face with Jean-Marc.

Time seems to stand still for a short moment. Emotions well up within me as I see him standing there, his familiar face etched with years of separation. Without a word, we embrace each other in the doorway, and in that moment, I feel a sense of coming home. The past is behind us, and the future stretches out before us, filled with so many possibilities.

My New Reality

W hile still entering piano competitions, I kept meeting with different masters, one of whom was Olivier Cazal. He is one of the most impressive persons I have ever met. He has participated in so many piano competitions and garnered so many prizes but he is so humble. He chose to stay in his little village, teach in a conservatory, and look after his family.

I played for him twice and he was so straightforward. He has no time for diplomacy. If you play well, he will tell you that you have done a good job. However, if you play badly, he will also let you know. In my case, he broke me into tiny pieces. Olivier Cazal and I spent many hours talking—I am very thankful for him being so honest at the time. Back then, I could be quite pig-headed. I would think that I played well and I was quite competitive. But his feedback helped me to grow. I feel that it helped me to become more of an artist. It's not about how fast I play or how accurate I am at the keyboard; it's about how I create. How I am able to connect with the audience. You don't have to be the best—and in any case, what is the best? Everyone has a different taste. Not every country likes to eat bread; some like rice, some like noodles, everyone is different, and so, who really determines who's the best? As musicians, we all have our own capabilities and that's perfectly okay.

Being in music school, you are bound to face difficulties. That and a LOT of competition. Everyone has to be the best and too many believe that to 'be the best,' they have to work on the demise of others. I have never understood that or involved myself in it. I have always focussed on myself and getting better. I was always my biggest competition. How do I get better than what I was during my last concert? How do I improve my own playing; outdo myself? My focus was always on myself and my own music. I always wanted to be a better version of myself. It's quite sad because jealousy and the fighting kills the market and the music. After all these years, after everything that I have been through, I value the music inside me even more. My own connection with music and how I translate that to the listener is what matters to me and by being better each time to ensure that I communicate that music to them.

I once saw Jean-Marc with a poster of Chopin sitting outside a concert hall in tears, holding a certificate for fourth price. It's written "The International Chopin Piano Competition." I found it so profound and political. It resonated with me: Chopin who was so great and had achieved so much continues to be surpassed in skills by so many young pianists today. So many pianists after him have gone on to play better than him. It proves that there is really no such thing as being the best. I told myself that even a young nobody like me could become the great concert pianist that I was aspiring to be.

Not long after seeing that poster, I read something written by Béla Bartók that says, "Competitions are for horses, not artists." I wasn't a horse. It made me reconsider my journey as a pianist. It made me rethink whether I wanted to continue on my path of partaking in competitions. I had already had doubts and this confirmed that I needed to pursue more than winning competitions. I'd turned down Sylvia's offer and left Singapore with the dream of becoming a concert pianist and it was about time that this became my focus, and so I dove right in and made that my career.

I love playing in concerts and exploring the different places that I travel to; that's a fact. However, it did and continues to take its toll on many aspects of my life. Let me pause here to tell you that becoming an artist requires a lot of sacrifices and hard work. You won't always find time for the people you love and that can be hard to deal with for both you and them—I've been there, more times than I want to admit. One day, while lying on my back in the pool, I asked myself, "Why do I keep travelling so much, going to all these places to play? I have to travel hours, sometimes days to get to some countries. I live on an island, so many people would love to visit it; why don't I bring everyone here to the island?" I looked up at the sky and saw the idea of piano island— bringing the piano to the island. I ran with the idea. I went to Paris and bought my very first Steinway piano. I got the Model D Concert Grand Piano, the biggest concert size piano, and shipped it to the island.

My friend, Jeremy, was still living in Australia. I called him and told him about my idea of hosting the piano festival. Jeremy has always been business minded and he's pretty much my big brother, so I knew I could count on him to help me develop this idea. Afterall, he had arranged my very first piano concert and we had made money from it when I was only fourteen. Now both of us were grownups and had acquired so much skills over the years, I knew we could pull off the festival as a team. Jeremy got on board with the idea of the piano festival and wanted to be part of it. I hosted the first festival in Singapore and flew Jeremy home to help me with it. It was the first time we had seen each other in eight years but it wouldn't be the last. On this trip, I decided to stay for an additional six days in Singapore. We had booked Jeremy's ticket for five days after the concert to give us time to reconnect and spend time with each other. I told everyone that I wasn't going to be in Singapore after the last night of the festival because I wanted time to catch up with my big brother. We had been apart for far too long.

On this trip, Jeremy learned more about me being homeless in Paris and apologised for not being able to help me when I had called him. I could tell that he felt guilty about it but I assured him that I wasn't angry. I completely understood. I knew that he would not have said no to me if he could have helped. Even on this trip, he gave me two thousand Singaporean dollars though I wasn't in need. I never held a grudge because I know he really cares for me. He's always looked after me as a little brother, so I had no hangups on him saying he couldn't help me once. Finding out that he was also going through so much at the time, there was no way I could be angry with him. I mean, he had been alone in Australia for eight years. His father refused to let him come home to Singapore, always telling him to stay in Australia and not come back to "make trouble for the family." For eight years, he never even left Australia for a holiday. Even before knowing this, I couldn't be angry with him. Jeremy remains part of my management team and continues to help me build my career. Now that this event in Singapore was a success, I could go bigger—it was time to bring everyone to the Réunion island.

Đặng Thái Sơn was one of my childhood heroes. I got the boldest of all ideas and decided to invite him to the 2nd Piano Island Festival. I felt so honoured when he responded saying that he would want to discover the island and he would love to come to the festival. Đặng Thái Sơn had agreed to come to the island because when the French invaded Vietnam, the last emperor of Vietnam was exiled to the Réunion in fear that he would start a revolution and reclaim the country as his own. Strangely enough, through the church I attend with my wife, we are friendly with the granddaughter, Dorothy, of that same emperor. For Đặng Thái Sơn, this is a very important connection because his mother is the founder of the first ever piano school in Vietnam. She knew the family of the emperor.

I was super excited to be bringing everyone to the island but at one point, it looked as though the festival wouldn't be a success. France went through a lot of social instability prior to Covid—the Yellow Vests Protests. People were very angry with the government. As a result, nothing was coming into the island. It lasted three weeks and everything was closed for those three weeks. The entire island was handicapped. It was a month before the concert was to take place that the protests started and this caused a lot of uncertainties. Everything was cut off. Then, as things normally work out for me these days, the week of the concert, they started to remove some of the roadblocks. The 2nd Piano Island Festival took place.

I was able to get Đặng Thái Sơn to meet Dorothy and this was important for him. He was then able to show this photo to his mother who was one hundred and three years old at the time. For me, it was a great honour spending time with my childhood hero. It meant so much to be driving him around the island for the ten days that he was there. We had a great time together.

Experiences like this drove me to create more festivals. These festivals are successful because I am known to take care of my artists, which is very important to me. Piano Island was the first festival I created and I have gone on to island hop to bring the music to different islands. I later on founded another festival in Europe, which I took to Faro this year—July 2023. I have a career playing concerts all over the world and now I have my own piano school.

For many years, my dream was to participate in The International Chopin Piano Competition, which happens once every five years. This is like the Olympics of the piano world. Chopin was my idol and I wanted more than anything to participate and win. The first time I was supposed to perform there, my teacher said I was too young, so I couldn't participate. The second time, I was twenty-three and I was getting married and still couldn't compete. Then the third time, the world was experiencing the Covid-19 pandemic. Now, I am too old and will never be able to participate in it. The age limit is thirty two and I am already thirty-one.

The amazing thing though is that I don't need to do that anymore; I have been able to achieve what I wanted to without it. I still have a long way to go but today I am living out my dream of being a concert pianist. Now I know that the biggest competition in the world is life itself—sometimes to get to the next day is the biggest challenge, and when you do it, it's the biggest achievement. Of course, I am saying this now from a very comfortable place in my life but if we are to look back on my life then, I am sure no one would have thought that I'd go this far in life let alone in my career. There were days when my biggest achievement was simply waking up alive the next day.

When President Macron first became president, every French National Day, he would invite a special guest from a different country. Most of whom were country leaders—prime ministers and presidents. In 2018, President Macron invited Prime Minister Lee Hsien Loong of Singapore as the guest of honour that year. At the time, I was quite close with the Embassy of the Republic of Singapore in Paris as I had been doing a few events with them. Ambassador Zainal Arif Mantaha, who I was acquainted with, had taken a liking to and got along with, invited me to play for the Prime Minister, which was a great honour. Unfortunately, I didn't get to meet Macron who was watching the World Cup Semi Finals, where France was playing against Belgium, so he wasn't there for the dinner. There were many other French ministers and delegates at the dinner. I played Liszt, Chopin, and Debussy.

I remember there being about four to five hundred people but the space made it feel far more intimate. The event was hosted at a very chic, luxurious restaurant near the Eiffel Tower. Channel News Asia also flew in, all the way from Singapore, to cover the event. I recall the Prime Minister walking to the stage, and before getting there, he stopped to shake my hand. What also amazed me was how protected he was. There were so many bodyguards guarding him—I think there were seven of them. We took a selfie but I couldn't hug him. There were two guards shielding him from my embrace. I had no right to touch him but it was good to see that he was willing to take a selfie with me. I found this experience all so profound in many ways. In some regard, the way people wanted to reach out and touch him reminded me of Jesus in the Bible and how people always wanted to reach out and touch Him when He was in their presence.

The most amazing part of this whole experience for me, however, was how in one moment, it was as though everything had come full circle. From me feeling as though I was going to combust in Singapore and wanting to get out, not being supported by my family in my wanting to become a pianist, the fight with my family that caused me to leave before I had planned to, how my mother struggled to get the help we needed for me to defer going into the National Service, being in Paris and seeing my dream of becoming a pianist almost slip through my fingers, being cold and homeless on the streets without food, without a way out, to becoming a concert pianist and living out my dream.

Everything came rushing to me and it all felt worth it when my Prime Minister said, "I know that you were playing Debussy because I know *Clair de Lune.*" I thought, *Wow, at least the Prime Minister of my country recognised the music I was playing.* Up to that point, I didn't think anyone was listening to me playing the piano. The space was extremely noisy as everyone was in awe of the Prime Minister being there. They were talking the whole time I played, so I never imagined anyone was really listening. However, in that moment, I felt hope. Hope for classical music in Singapore. Hope that there will come a time when a Singaporean child choosing to become an artist of any sort will be supported by not only their families but also Singaporean society. Hope that careers in the arts will one day be seen as viable career options.

I am not quite ready to end my story—life is still happening for me—or tell you about everything that's happened since 2022. I think I want to save that for when I talk about the second half of my life. Even though I have been through so much, like being homeless, losing so much weight because I didn't have enough food, those are physical things and they are survivable. However, I have not always been the person to get through emotional struggles easily— those are the things that always threaten to break me. I am the child who cries for seemingly nothing. I feel a lot and I can't seem to handle matters of the heart very well. I am writing this book because I want everyone out there to know that we can keep going, no matter what we have been through. If you have a dream for your life and work hard at it, you can make that dream a reality. It won't always be easy but maybe it shouldn't be.

I don't want to relive the life of my father. Maybe I'll bring you up to speed on that later in another book. I am also not yet ready to disclose that aspect of my life yet, either—there are still too many moving parts.

I am open to the future, and whatever comes, I am ready to face it. If someone as ordinary as me could go through everything and still become successful, I think anyone can do it and that is what I want you to take away from this book.

With Prime Minister Lee Hsien Loong of Singapore at the
French National Day event

With HE Zainal Mantaha, Ambassador of Singapore to
France, in 2017

Trying out a new piano in a new hall

With my teacher, Jean-Marc Luisada, after his successful
concert, where I turned the page for him at my own festival

266

At a piano concert in Réunion, 2023

At a concert in Steinway & Sons, Beijing

Jury member at the Vivace International Piano Competition

Performing at the competition's closing ceremony

With Minister of State, Ms Sim Ann, at the presentation of
the 3rd Piano Island Festival in Singapore

Singaporean pianist Wang Congyu now a Steinway Artist

Shannon Ling

Singaporean pianist Wang Congyu was only 16 when he left school to pursue music in Paris.

"It was a very bold move and everyone around me was very much against it," says the 30-year-old, who is now based in Reunion Island, which is in the Indian Ocean, close to Africa.

He was selected for a scholarship to attend Ecole Normale de Musique de Paris. Moving to Paris without much parental support, however, meant that he struggled both financially and mentally.

After going through tough times – including living on the streets and making a living by playing music in bars – he has made a mark in the classical music scene.

He is the founder and artistic director of the Piano Island Festival and was recently named a Steinway Artist.

These artists are chosen to perform on Steinway pianos exclusively. Wang joins the likes of Chinese pianist Lang Lang, Argentinian classical pianist Martha Argerich and American singer-songwriter Charlie Puth. Singaporean pianist Benjamin Loh is also on the roster.

"I was really, really delighted when I got the news via e-mail," says Wang, who was a Young Steinway Artist for about 10 years. "I've been asking for a couple of years now to convert to Steinway Artist, but each time, something would happen, not necessarily to me, but to the world, like the pandemic."

He says the conversion depends on the merits of one's career. With his concerts and shows back on after being postponed or cancelled during the pandemic, he was nominated a Steinway Artist.

During the earlier part of the pandemic, he took in more piano students, teaching them virtually via platforms such as WhatsApp, Zoom and Instagram.

His dream is to develop the next generation of musicians in Southeast Asia. This drove him to create the Piano Island Festival in 2017, which aims to give young musicians a chance to learn from professionals and interact with music enthusiasts.

Mr Jeremy Yeo, 35, who manages the festival, says: "Our motto is always to live your dream. It is not about doing what other people want you to do, but also doing what you like."

This year will be the fifth edition of the festival, which the organisers say is the biggest in terms of the number of teachers and students, as well as the size of the venue and quality of pianos used.

The plan is to take in at least 80 to 100 students, an increase from about 40 in previous years.

Wang says: "We haven't done a physical festival since 2019 so we have been saving all of our energy and resources to make this festival a huge one."

The first part of the event is a series of concerts in Singapore in October, titled French Piano Series. Apart from Wang, French pianist Jean-Marc Luisada and Japanese pianist Hayato Sumino will also be performing at the Victoria Concert Hall.

After that is a festival with students in December, to be held in Kuala Lumpur, Malaysia.

"I haven't played in Singapore since 2015," says Wang. "So, I very much look forward to playing in Singapore again during my homecoming concert."

FRENCH PIANO SERIES

WHERE Victoria Concert Hall, 11 Empress Place
WHEN Oct 9 (Jean-Marc Luisada), Oct 11 (Wang Congyu), Oct 12 (Hayato Sumino); 7.30pm
ADMISSION $40 to $150, tickets on sale from July 4 at ticketmaster.sg
INFO pianoislandfestival.com

Article about my becoming a Steinway Artist

A masterclass with young students at Steinway Singapore, 2022

Playing at a concert in Sant Pere de Rodes, the famous Benedictine monastery in Catalonia, Spain, where *Game of Thrones* was filmed

Concert in the Réunion with Benjamin after not playing
together for ten years

EPILOGUE

I STROLL DOWN IMP. DE la Baleine then turn left onto Rue Jean-Pierre. I walk past shop after the shop making my way to The Hood Paris. I am stopping in for a quick bite and to see my friend, Pearlyn. Across the street, I admire graffiti painted on a downed shutter but quickly pull my attention back to watching where I am going. It's just like it was the last time I was here. There's a chalkboard outside advertising today's specials. There is a menu in the window showcasing everything that's on offer and colourful containers can be seen in the window.

I step into the restaurant. It's a little busy inside.

"Hello, hello," I greeted everyone. Immediately, Pearlyn's colleague yelled for her to come see me, telling her that her friend is here.

I wait for her to come out and she doesn't take long.

"Hi Pearlyn, so good to see you again," I greeted her. "How have you been?"

"It's always good to see you. I am good, very good. A little hot at the minute but what else can you expect in the middle of July in Paris?" We both chuckle. "Anyway, how are you? Here for another concert?"

"Yeah, it's very hot. At least it's a little cooler in here. I've been well. And yes, you know me well. I am playing a concert this week, but I also have some other business that I need to handle while I am here."

"Busy as always. Busy as always. What else are you up to now?"

"I'm actually in the process of finishing my book and that's taking a lot of my attention these days."

"Aw yes, you said you were doing that. I knew there was something I wanted to run by you. So, Sharon Au is here this week. I mean, you always come when she's not around. And Anthony as well, the film director. He's also around this week, so we should have a dinner."

"Okay. I don't mind. Where shall we go?" She looks around her restaurant as if to ask what I mean. "Aw, you mean we should come here for dinner?"

"That's exactly what I mean. Let's get together and eat good Singaporean food."

"Okay, I'd like that. It would be good to meet them both, and of course, eat good food."

"Meet them? I don't just want you to meet them, I want you to share your story with them so that they can make a movie about it!"

I chuckled.

"No, no, Congyu. This is no joke. You shouldn't just stop at it being a book. You should…"

"I don't take it as a joke. I just don't know…"

"Let's just meet them and see what happens. No need to make a decision now."

I Am Congyu

M y name is Congyu and I am a concert pianist. I've dedicated almost my entire life to mastering the piano, and it's an ongoing journey. With each note I play, I inch closer to the greatness I've always aspired to.

For me, being intelligent is not just about being able to study and secure your place in traditional careers like being a doctor or an engineer; it's about being resourceful, learning from every experience, and evolving. It's about becoming successful. A very studious child isn't intelligent if they can't use the resources they have or can access to become successful.

It's about learning how to be the best at what you love by learning what it takes and putting that knowledge to good use. That is what I have done.

I might not be a musical genius, but I'm smart enough to know that luck, hard work, and dedication can bridge the gap. Talent is important but it's only one percent of the equation. To be intelligent is to know that you have to work hard. You have to be dedicated to nurturing that talent as it won't do anything on its own. Thus, I would say that hard work and dedication makes up another nine percent of the equation.

I am smart enough to know that majority of one's success, the remaining ninety percent, comes down to luck.

You have to be in the right place at the right time. To make the right connections.

I am living out my name every day, embracing my parents' expectations in my own way. François Weigel's words resonate deeply within me: I connect the brilliance of virtuosity with the delicate poetry of music, crafting my unique path.

I am Congyu Wang, and I am intelligent and great at what I am passionate about. The piano. Of course, I can learn to play better, and I am working on that every day. In the meantime, with each step in that direction, I know that my name is not just a label; it's a promise I'm determined to fulfil.

My homecoming concert at the Victoria Theatre and
Concert Hall in Singapore 2022

Acknowledgements

Writing this memoir has been cathartic, and I am profoundly grateful to the many individuals who have played pivotal roles in shaping my life and career. To each and every one of you, thank you for being a part of my story.

First and foremost, Julie Wang, my wife, deserves special mention for her support and love, for choosing to stay by my side through the toughest moments.

To my mother, who not only gave me life but also instilled in me the principles of being a good person, thank you for your guidance and love.

Huiqi, my sister, has been the best example any brother could ask for, always pushing me forward to take the next leap. ZhiWei, my brother, deserves appreciation for tolerating all my nonsense and showering me with love and support from the day he was born.

Jeremy Yeo, you have been the big brother I never had, always there to encourage me in the toughest of times. I am grateful for your constant support.

Patrick and Joanne, my parents-in-law, thank you for your love and support. Benjamin Brandeleer Ligeer, your friendship, support, and care have meant the world to me.

Wayne Teo, you are the best company and will forever be a treasured friend. Jesse Lai, thank you for your friendship and the stories from National Service.

John and Rebecca, you are my spiritual parents, and your care and support have been invaluable. Xiu Lan, David, Phillipe, and Nicolas, the family who took me in during my darkest days, thank you for loving me like your own.

Nerissa Chen, your friendship is truly appreciated. Zara Monica, thank you for your friendship and trust.

Li Si, thanks for all the treats in Paris and for being my big brother. Gu Yue, your restaurant tickets were a lifesaver!

Daim Dean, thank you for teaching me how to use the electric keyboard. Irsyad Alif, you made time pass much faster during National Service.

Neville Athenasius, your friendship and our musical adventures during National Service are unforgettable. Noah Zhou and Vasco Dantas, your contributions to the piano concerto festival and this book are deeply appreciated.

Celine Goh, thanks for nominating me as a Young Steinway Artist. Andrew Goh, your trust and friendship during the Young Steinway Artist nomination meant a lot; thanks for your continued support.

Sharon Au, my childhood television hero, who inspired me to write this book; thank you. Anthony Chen, your ideas and advice for this book were invaluable. Pearlyn Lee, thanks for your friendship and for creating the amazing restaurant 'The Hood' in Paris (my canteen) and for introducing me to the people I should have met in Paris ages ago.

Jean-Marc Luisada, my master, thank you for teaching me everything about music and life. Gabriel Tacchino, rest well, teacher. You were a great friend and musical advisor.

To Kemone for your contributions to this book, the many late night interviews over the phone and WhatsApp and for making this book possible.

François Weigel, thank you for believing in me and giving me my first public recital in France. Éric Heidsieck, your influence in my music is immeasurable.

Jean Paul Sevilla, thanks for your advice in my musical career. Odile Catelin-Delangle, you were the most patient teacher.

Ádám György, you were an inspiration in my teenage years, and I am grateful for your advice. Igor Lasko, you taught me that everything is possible with music.

France Clidat and Sergio Peticaroli, your precious advice in my playing will always stay close to my heart. Rest well.

Aquiles Delle Vigne, thank you for the wonderful conversations about Arrau, Cziffra, and Magda Tagliaferro. Carles and Sofia, for believing in me and helping produce my first album.

H.E. Zainal Mantaha, thank you for trusting me with many National Day performances and for the opportunities and friendship.

Gerrit Glaner, for appointing me Steinway Artist in 2022. Steinway & Sons, for producing the best pianos in the world.

Rachel and Julian, thank you both for your contributions to recommend this book. Boo Kok Chuon, your support and advice whilst writing this book has been invaluable; thank you.

To Lawrence Lee, thank you for your support and the promotion of this book.

Seabourn, for the wonderful memories with some of the world's greatest travellers. Handre Potgieter, thank you for your friendship and for helping me realize my dream of performing on cruises.

To everyone mentioned here, and to those I may have inadvertently missed, your impact on my life is immeasurable, and I am truly grateful for your presence and contributions.

Finally, to Singapore, Paris, and the Réunion island, for shaping me into the man and musician I am today. My love for each of you will outlive my lifespan. Thank you for all the opportunities and the countless memories that I will forever cherish… And the opportunity to make even more.

About the Cover

On August 9, 2015, Singapore celebrated its fiftieth National Day, marking half a century since gaining independence from Malaysia in 1965. In celebration, the government purchased a red Steinway piano. It was the first red grand concert piano in the world, known as 'The Red Pops,' and was created by Steinway & Sons in collaboration with Chinese artist and designer, Zao Wou-Ki. It went on a world tour to a total of twenty-two countries before it headed back to Singapore and was purchased by the National Museum of Singapore. It was displayed as part of the museum's collection, allowing visitors to appreciate the artistic and musical significance of the instrument in the context of Singapore's cultural heritage.

I got the opportunity to play on the piano for the first time while it was housed at the museum. Then, earlier this year in 2023, it was sent to Steinway in Singapore for maintenance. Steinway offered to let me come play and teach some lessons on the piano. I thought I couldn't miss the opportunity to not only play but also be photographed with it, so I got my friend, Esther, to come take some photos with me and The Red Pops. When the photos were shown to me, I thought the one that now graces this cover was just perfect as a book cover.

My first time playing on The Red Pops

Another photo from that shoot with The Red Pops

About the Pianist

Hailed as a "complete musician — a sensitive artist and an extremely talented young pianist," Congyu Wang is an internationally renowned soloist who has garnered acclaim as a recitalist, accompanist, and chamber musician.

Born in Singapore, Congyu started playing the piano at the age of three, receiving instruction from different masters, until he later came under the tutelage of Sylvia Ng. He was selected for a scholarship that enabled him to attend the prestigious École Normale de Musique de Paris, where he studied with renowned French pianists, Jean-Marc Luisada and Odile Catelin-Delangle. He later enrolled in La Schola Cantorum (Paris) to continue his studies with Gabriel Tacchino, who had been Francis Poulenc's only student. From an early age, Congyu has enjoyed phenomenal success in international piano competitions, ultimately winning the Grand Prize in Berlin and Bordeaux. His other prizes include Vulaines-sur-Seine, Lagny-sur-Marne, Merignac, Paris, Jakarta, Tallinn, and Cle d'Or Reunion. He was featured in the national news journal 'Zao Bao' as Singapore's most promising young artist of the year in 2016. In 2022, he won the Germaine Mounier Prix and 2nd Prize at the Albert Roussel International Piano Competition in Paris.

At the Chopin International Piano Competition for Young Pianists in Slovenia, Congyu was awarded 6th Prize. One of the jury members, François Weigel, believed he should have won, and resigned thereupon in protest. Congyu has since made appearances in over 800 recitals in France, England, Italy, Spain, Portugal, Belgium, Switzerland, Germany, Croatia, Estonia, Finland, Sweden, Latvia, Mauritius, South

Africa, Reunion Island, China, Thailand, Indonesia, Malaysia, Singapore, and other countries.

Highlights of some of his performances include festival appearances at Château de la Verrerie (France), Ernen Music Festival (Switzerland), the Geza Anda Piano Festival Masterclasses (Berlin), the International Isang Yun Academy (Paris), International Hammer Klavier Piano Series (Barcelona), International Piano Festival (Amarante), Festival Langtang (Reunion Island), and Chopin Fest (Belgrade). Congyu has captivated audiences worldwide, performing for an array of distinguished guests, including celebrities, bankers, diplomats, and ambassadors from France, Singapore, China, and Norway, as well as the Prince of Brunei and the Prime Minister of Singapore.

Congyu has earned a reputation for delivering stunning performances of extremely demanding repertoire. His vast repertoire includes 30 piano concertos, along with the complete solo piano oeuvre of Chopin and Poulenc. He has shared the stage with many well-known musicians, such as Roman Leuleu, Agnes Kallay, Giancarlo de Lorenzo, Elena Xanthoudakis, Grigor Palikarov, Quatour Arsis, etc.

In 2015, Congyu published his first album *Charme* on KNS classical, featuring the works of Francis Poulenc to international acclaim. Recently, he released his second album *Reflets*, dedicated to Claude Debussy, commemorating the 100th death anniversary of the French Composer. His recordings are frequently broadcasted on radios internationally – France Musique, BBC Radio 3 (UK), Radio Vie (Reunion), Radio Antena 2 (Portugal), Classic 1027 (South Africa), Symphony 92.4 (Singapore), etc.

He was featured on the movie *Une Barque sur l'Ocean,* directed by French director, Arnold de Parscau in 2019.

He is also the Founder and Artistic Director of the Piano Island Festival, Piano Concerto Festival, and the International Chopin Competition in South Africa. He is ambassador to several charitable foundations, including Association des Jeunes Musiciens (Young musicians), Association Koinonia (International Refugees), and Grace International Foundation Liverpool (Youth Development).

Congyu Wang is a Steinway Artist.

Connect with Congyu on Instagram: @wang_congyu

Awards and Recognition

2016	Grand Prix Cle d'Or La Reunion
	Second Prize Alion Baltic International Music
2015	Competition, Estonia
2014	SCDF Service Excellence Award
2013	Third Prize at the Ananda Sukarlan Award, Indonesia
	Young Steinway Artist Title
2012	Second Prize at Concours des Etoiles de Paris
2011	Grand Prix at the Merignac Concours
	Semi-finalist at Concours de Chatou
	Semi-finalist at Piano Campus International Piano Competition
	Special Mention at Lagny sur Marne Concours International
	Second Prize at Vulaines sur Seine Concours de piano (No First Prize awarded)
2010	Semi-finalist at the Adilia Alieva Competition in Gaillard
	Grand Prize at Berlin International Piano Competition "Sforzando'
	1st Prize at Bordeaux European youth competition

Major Teachers

Piano
Jean-Marc Luisada
Ádám György
Odile Catelin-Delangle
Gabriel Tacchino
François Weigel
Éric Heidsieck
Sylvia Ng
Igor Lasko

Chamber Music
Nina Patarcec
Marchais Christine

Master Classes
France Clidat
Sergio Perticaroli
Aquiles Delle Vigne
Françoise Thinat
Pietro de Maria
Kaya Han
Nicolas Ong
Elena Nesterenko
Jean-Paul Sevilla
Đặng Thái Sơn
Vladimir Vlado
Lily Dorfman

Upcoming Concerts

**For exact concert dates, please visit www.congyuwang.com

December 2023	Rachmaninoff Piano Concerto in Reunion Island
	Rachmaninoff Piano Concerto in Jakarta, Indonesia
	Piano Recital in Singapore
January 2024	Piano Concert in Manila, Philippines
	Piano Concert in Shenzhen, China
	Piano Concert in Taiwan
February 2024	Piano Concert in Mauritius
	Piano Recital in Grosetto, Italy
March 2024	Rachmaninoff Piano Concerto in Singapore
	Concert Tour in China
	Piano Concert in Manila–Hanoi (Seabourn)
April 2024	Piano Concert in Grenoble, France
	Piano Concert in California, USA
	Piano Concert Arrecife–Ibiza–Barcelona, Spain (Seabourn)
June 2024	Piano Concerto Festival in Grosetto, Italy
July 2024	Piano Concerto Festival in Faro, Portugal
	Piano Concerto Festival in Osimo, Italy
	Piano Island Festival in Jakarta, Indonesia
August 2024	Piano Island Competition in Singapore

September 2023 Piano Concert in Reykjavik, Iceland (Seabourn)
Piano Concert Dubrovnik (Seabourn)

Milton Keynes UK
Ingram Content Group UK Ltd.
UKHW041921091223
434097UK00001B/1